Grades 1–6

Gotta Have Graphs!

35 Kid-Pleasing, Curriculum-Based Graphing and Data Displays

Table of Contents

www.themailbox.com

©2003 The Education Center, Inc.
All rights reserved.
ISBN10 #1-56234-573-7 • ISBN13 #978-156234-573-0

Manufactured in the United States
10 9 8 7 6 5 4 3

About This Book

   Gotta Have Graphs! makes real-life math fun and easy. The book is divided into 13 different sections, each focusing on a different type of graph or data display. Every section contains two or three four-page lessons. Each lesson contains step-by-step directions for introducing the graphing activity as well as for collecting, displaying, and discussing the data. Lessons also contain an additional idea for further extending the graphing activity if desired. Preparation for each graphing activity is a breeze, and the graphing activities use easy-to-obtain data. Easy-to-follow teacher instructions are provided as well as sample illustrations of completed graphs and data displays. Activities within each section of the book are presented in order of difficulty so you can quickly pick the lesson that best meets the needs of your students. The completed graphs provide eye-catching and thought-provoking displays with plenty of opportunities for student interpretation. It's skill building, it's easy, and it's fun. You've gotta have graphs!

Types of Graphs Featured in This Book

Object Graph
Object graphs (sometimes called real graphs) are created using actual objects. The object graphs in this book are appropriate for grades 1–4.

Picture Graph
Picture graphs (sometimes called pictographs) are constructed using magazine pictures, photographs, or illustrations to represent real things. The picture graphs in this book are appropriate for grades 1–4.

Symbolic Graph
Symbolic graphs are constructed using symbols, such as tally marks or sticky notes, that represent the items being graphed. The symbol graphs in this book are appropriate for grades 1–6.

Line Plot
Line plots show whether data is all bunched up or spread out. Range and mode can quickly be identified in line plots. A line plot shows numerical data plotted as Xs above numbers on a number line. The line plots in this book are appropriate for grades 1–6.

Bar Graph
Bar graphs use vertical or horizontal parallel bars to compare information from several categories. The bar graphs in this book are appropriate for grades 1–6.

Line Graph
Line graphs display continuous data. This type of graph shows how things change over time. The line graphs in this book are appropriate for grades 3–6.

Types of Graphs Featured in This Book
(continued)

Circle Graph
Circle graphs (sometimes called pie charts) are used when data indicates a comparison of parts to a whole. The circle graphs in this book are appropriate for grades 3–6.

Stem-and-Leaf Plot
In a stem-and-leaf plot, the numerical data is organized so that the numbers themselves make the display. The stem-and-leaf plots in this book are appropriate for grades 4–6.

Histogram
Histograms are bar graphs that show the number of times (frequency) data occurs within intervals. The bars in a histogram are connected rather than separated as in a regular bar graph. The histograms in this book are appropriate for grade 6.

Box-and-Whisker Plot
Box-and-whisker plots (sometimes called box plots) display how far apart and how evenly data are distributed. The middle 50 percent of a set of data values is boxed in. The lines (whiskers) stemming from the left and right sides of the box represent the lower 25 percent and the upper 25 percent of the numbers for the set of data values. The vertical line inside the box represents the median (the middle number) of the entire set of data. The first vertical line of the box represents the lower median (first quartile). The last vertical line of the box represents the upper median (third quartile). The box plots in this book are appropriate for grade 6.

Other Data Displays Featured in This Book

Glyph
Glyphs are pictorial displays of information. Each detail of the picture represents a different piece of information. The glyphs in this book are appropriate for grades 1–6.

Venn Diagram
A Venn diagram is a set of interlocking circles that shows relationships between sets of objects. The Venn diagrams in this book are appropriate for grades 1–6.

Timeline
A timeline is a display that is a number line. The numbers on the number line represent some measure of time, such as hours, days, or years. Past events can be plotted on a timeline. Timelines can also show events planned for the future. The timelines in this book are appropriate for grades 1–6.

Graphing "Pasta-bilities"

Serve up a heaping helping of learning with this object graph activity!

Materials

- copy of page 6 for each student
- copy of the plate pattern on page 7 for each student
- one box each of uncooked rigatoni, wheel, and twist pasta
- large bowl
- 3 oz. cup for each student
- tape
- crayons
- glue

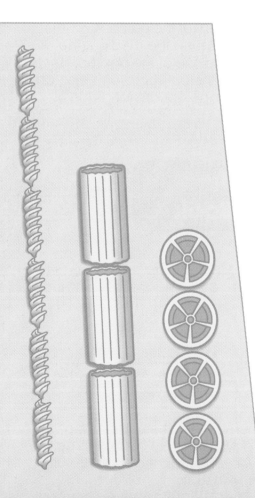

1. Introduce It!

For a "pasta-tively" delightful beginning, explain to students that an *object graph* is used to organize data with real objects. The objects must be the same size and shape or be placed on equal-sized spaces. Then tell students that they will be making object graphs with uncooked pasta.

2. Collect It!

Give each student a cup and a copy of page 6. Show students the three different types of pasta and share the name of each one. Then combine the pasta in one large bowl. Invite each child to scoop a cupful of pasta and then return to her seat.

3. Display It! Discuss It!

Instruct each child to study the graph on page 6. Ask students to consider why there are boxes for the pasta. To help students understand why, direct each child to sort her pasta pieces into rows on her desk. Point out that since the pasta pieces are different sizes, a longer row might make it look as if there were more pieces (see illustration on page 4). Further explain that placing the pieces in same-size boxes makes it easier to compare how many there are of each type.

Next, have each child sort her pasta pieces on the graph, beginning with the far left space of each row. When she has sorted her pasta correctly, direct her to glue each piece in place. Then use the provided questions to prompt a discussion about the results.

Name __Esther__   *Object graph*

Pasta Graph

Twist									
Rigatoni									
Wheel									

Questions

Which type of pasta appears the most? The least?

Look at a classmate's graph. How is your graph different? How is it alike?

What makes an object graph different from a picture or bar graph? *(It uses real objects instead of pictures or bars.)*

How might your graph look different if you took two cupfuls of pasta instead of one? *(There would probably be more pasta pieces in each row.)*

4. Extend It!

What is the most preferred pasta among your students? Find out with this picture graph activity. In advance, prepare a four-column graph on chart paper and label it as shown. To begin the activity, give each child a plate pattern from page 7. Read the question and choices aloud. Have each child draw her favorite pasta on the plate pattern and sign her name. If her choice is "None of these," tell her to draw the pasta that *is* her favorite or, if she doesn't like pasta at all, to leave the plate empty. Ask her to tape her plate to the appropriate column on the graph. Discuss the results as a class. Mmm...what a tasty graph!

Which is your favorite pasta?

Spaghetti	Lasagna	Ravioli	None of these

Pasta Graph

Twist									
Rigatoni									
Wheel									

©The Education Center, Inc. • Gotta Have Graphs! • TEC60780

Note to the teacher: Use with pages 4 and 5.

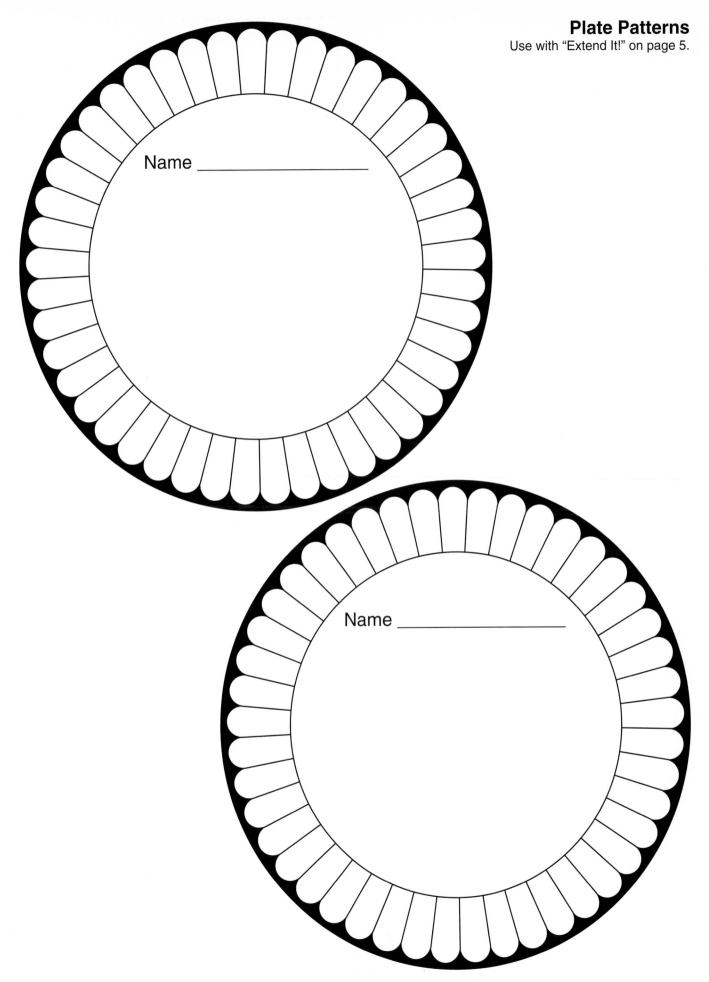

Name _____

Name _____

Size It Up!

This object graph activity is a perfect fit!

Materials

- copy of pages 10 and 11 for each student
- masking tape
- 3 sentence strips
- 15 index cards
- bulletin board paper
- scissors
- crayons
- glue

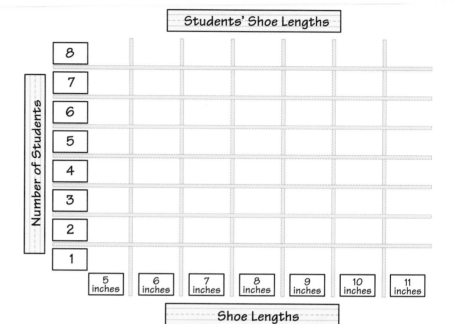

Students' Shoe Lengths

Number of Students: 8, 7, 6, 5, 4, 3, 2, 1

Shoe Lengths: 5 inches, 6 inches, 7 inches, 8 inches, 9 inches, 10 inches, 11 inches

1. Introduce It!

To kick off this activity, prepare for a floor graph using masking tape, index cards, and sentence strips as shown. Explain to students that an *object graph* compares data using real objects. Then tell students that they will construct an object graph to compare their shoe lengths.

2. Collect It!

Remind students that before they can make the object graph, they must first find out each shoe length. Give each student a copy of page 10. Have the child cut out the patterns and then glue them together where indicated. Instruct the student to remove his right shoe and measure its length in inches using the pattern. To do this, direct him to place the back of his shoe against the zero line and then trace the toe with a pencil. Have him use a crayon to trace the horizontal line closest to his shoe's toe mark.

Students' Shoe Lengths

Number of Students

| 8 |
| 7 |
| 6 |
| 5 |
| 4 |
| 3 |
| 2 |
| 1 |

5 inches · 6 inches · 7 inches · 8 inches · 9 inches · 10 inches · 11 inches

Shoe Lengths

3. Display It! Discuss It!

After each child has measured his shoe, instruct the class to sit in a circle around the floor graph, bringing his shoe and shoe pattern with him. In turn, ask each student to place his shoe in the column of the graph to indicate his shoe length.

Next, ask students to study the graph. Invite them to speculate why some shoe lengths were not included on the graph. *(It is unlikely that students would have certain shoe lengths because of their age.)* Then prompt students to compare the information on the graph by asking questions such as the following: How long are most students' shoes? What shoe length did the fewest students have? How many more students have seven-inch shoes than six-inch shoes? How many students have six-inch shoes and eight-inch shoes all together?

4. Extend It!

For further graphing practice that's sure to be a "shoe-in," have youngsters construct these picture graphs! On a large sheet of bulletin board paper, prepare a graph similar to the one shown, including one column for each shoe type. Explain that a picture graph is made using pictures, photographs, or illustrations to represent real things. Next, give each student a copy of page 11. Instruct the student to decide which type of shoe he is wearing, color the pattern, and then cut out the card. Invite each child to glue his shoe card in the appropriate column of the graph. Discuss the results as a class. Then use the questions below to help students compare the picture graph to the object graph previously created. Now that's some fancy footwork!

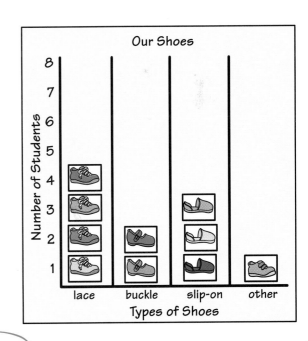

Our Shoes

Number of Students

| 8 |
| 7 |
| 6 |
| 5 |
| 4 |
| 3 |
| 2 |
| 1 |

lace · buckle · slip-on · other

Types of Shoes

Questions

How are the two graphs alike? *(They both display information about shoes.)*

How are the two graphs different? *(One graph displays shoe lengths; the other displays shoe types.)*

Which graph is better for sharing information with other people? *(Possible response: the picture graph because the shoes on the object graph must be returned)*

Which graph did you prefer making?

Shoe Length Pattern
Use with pages 8 and 9.

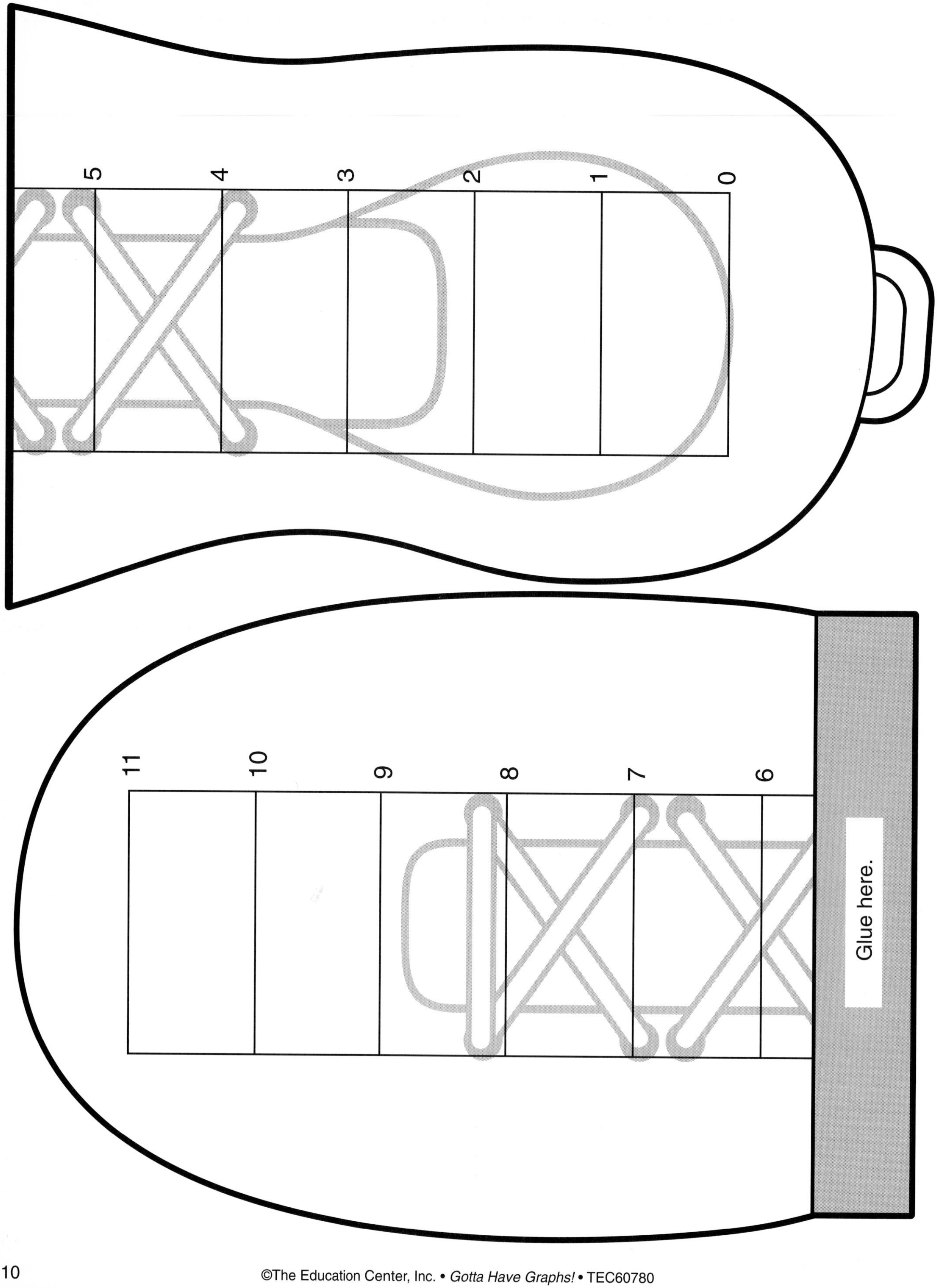

5 4 3 2 1 0

11 10 9 8 7 6

Glue here.

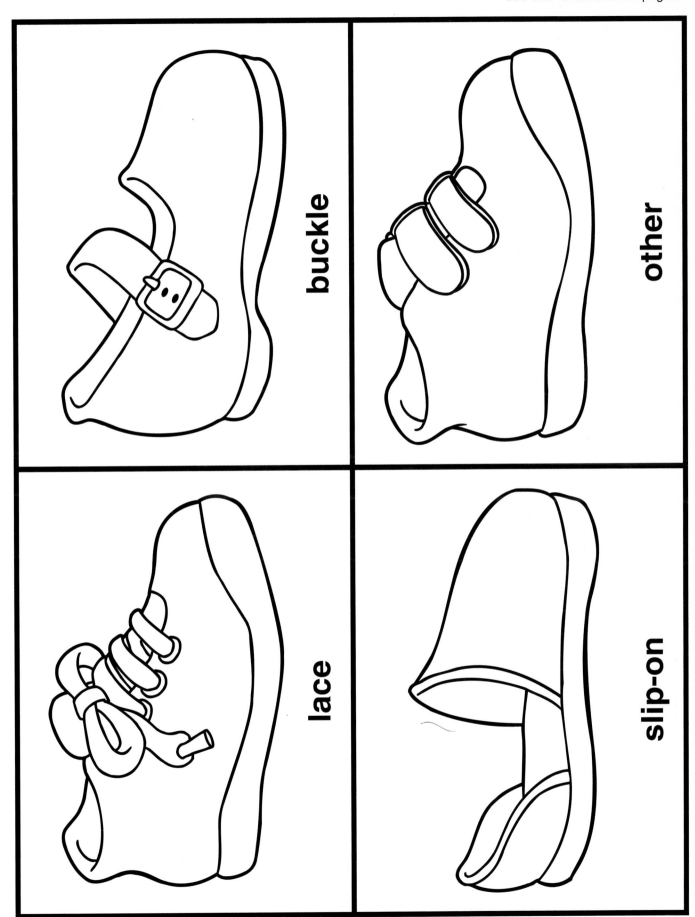

buckle

other

lace

slip-on

Activity #3

A Good-Tasting Graph

You can bet your students will experience sweet success making these object graphs!

Materials

- copy of pages 14 and 15 for each student
- 1 lb. bag of Smarties candy rolls (contains approximately 64 candy rolls)

Is there an equal number of each color in a roll of Smarties candies?	
Yes	No
Tasha	Judith
Ryan	Brian
Michele	Matt
Erica	Elena
Carla	Eddie
Melvin	

1. Introduce It!

Sweeten up your students' knowledge of *object graphs* by explaining that these types of graphs use real objects to organize data. Then tell students that they will be making object graphs using Smarties candy rolls. Draw a chart on the board similar to the one shown. Then open a roll of candies and review the six colors with students *(green, yellow, purple, pink, orange, and white)*. Next, ask each child to predict whether or not a roll of Smarties candies will contain an equal number of candies for each color. Then have her write her name in the appropriate column.

2. Collect It! Display It!

Give each child a copy of page 14 and a roll of Smarties candies. Have each student sort her candies by color and place them on the corresponding columns on the graph. Then, for each candy color, have her write the total number of candies on the provided line.

3. Discuss It!

Have students compare their results to the predictions made in "Introduce It!" on page 12. Then facilitate a discussion about the results using the questions shown. Help your students resist the temptation to dig in before completing the activity in "Extend It!" below.

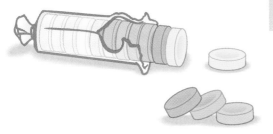

Questions

Is there an equal number of each color?
Which color has the most?
Which color has the least?
Which color has more: pink or green? How many more?
What is the fractional amount of each color?

4. Extend It!

Satisfy each student's sweet tooth with a bar graph activity that takes the previous data a step further. Based on the results from the object graph activity, ask students to predict which color will be the most prevalent in the large bag of Smarties candy rolls. Next, equally distribute the remaining candy rolls from the bag. (Set aside any extra candy rolls.) Direct each student to sort her candies by color and add them to the data on her object graph from "Collect It! Display It!" on page 12. Have students total each candy color and adjust the candy totals at the bottom of the reproducible.

In turn, have each student share her candy total for each color. As students share their totals, record their totals on the board. Then use a calculator to determine the grand total of each candy color and post these numbers on the board too. Next, have students use this information to complete a copy of page 15. After students complete the reproducible, lead a class discussion about the results. Then invite students to gobble the edible data. What a tasty conclusion!

Grand Totals for Each Candy Color

White	146
Pink	193
Purple	125
Yellow	137
Green	175
Orange	184

A Smart Graph

1. Sort your candies on the graph.

White	Yellow	Pink	Green	Purple	Orange

2. Write the total for each color.

White _____   Pink _____   Purple _____

Yellow _____   Green _____   Orange _____

The Color Appearing Most Often Is...

Complete the bar graph.

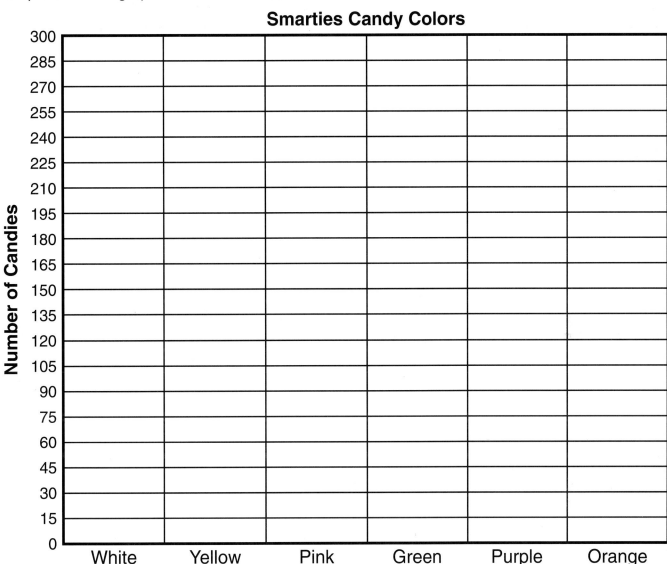

1. Which color appears most often? _____

2. Which color appears least often? _____

3. Create a title for this graph. _____

   _____

4. Write two sentences that provide additional information about the graph.

   _____

   _____

Cute As a Button!

Sew up students' graphing skills with this "fasten-ating" picture graph activity!

Materials for Each Student

- copy of page 18
- button pattern from page 19
- 12 buttons (in various sizes, shapes, and colors)
- loop of tape
- scissors
- crayons
- glue

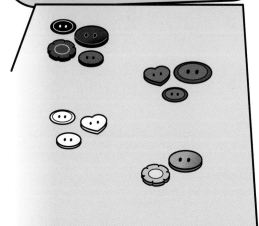

Size	Number of Holes	Shape	Color
small	one	square	white
medium	two	circle	black
large	four	triangle	brown
			red

1. Introduce It!

Button up students' knowledge of *picture graphs* by pointing out that a picture graph uses magazine pictures, photographs, or illustrations to represent information, instead of real objects. Then explain to students that they will construct picture graphs to display sets of buttons.

2. Collect It!

To begin, give each child 12 randomly selected buttons. Have students brainstorm various ways to sort their buttons, such as by size, shape, color, or number of holes. List students' attribute suggestions on the board to create column headings. With students' input, list the possible choices below each attribute. Then instruct each child to choose one of the attributes and sort his buttons accordingly. (If his attribute results in more than four groups, have him sort his buttons a different way.)

3. Display It! Discuss It!

After students finish sorting, give each child a copy of page 18. Point out that each button pattern stands for a real button. Then instruct each child to cut out the buttons on the page. Tell him to title his graph with the attribute and then write the categories he chose in the blocks at the bottom of the page. (Remind him that he does not need to use all the spaces.) Next, tell him to place his button cutouts on the graph to show the number of real buttons in each category. Then instruct him to glue the cutouts in place.

Next, invite students to share their completed graphs with the class. To do this, encourage each child to compare the buttons in two or more categories. (For example, he might say that he has two more white buttons than brown buttons.) Then use the provided questions for further discussion about the graphs.

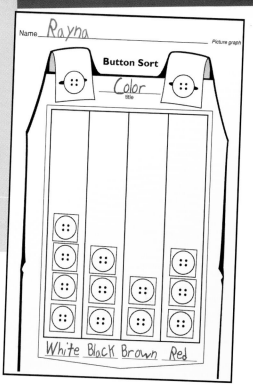

Questions

How are all the graphs different? *(They display information for different groups of buttons; students sorted the buttons in different ways.)*

How are the graphs alike? *(They all display information for the same number of buttons.)*

If all the students sorted their buttons by shape, how would the graphs be the same? How would they be different? *(Possible answer: The graphs would have been labeled the same, but they may have had different numbers of buttons in each column.)*

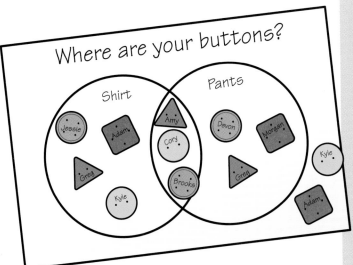

4. Extend It!

Have your youngsters disocver where buttons are located on their clothing with this Venn diagram activity. On the board, draw a large Venn diagram labeled as shown. Give each student a button pattern from page 19. Have him color and personalize it. Then ask students to predict by a show of hands where most students are wearing buttons—on their shirts, pants, both, or neither. Encourage students to explain the reasoning behind their predictions. Next, tell each student to search his clothes for any buttons. Invite him to tape his button pattern to the Venn diagram to indicate the location of any buttons. (If a child is not wearing buttons or is wearing something other than a shirt and pants, the cutout should be taped outside of the sets.) After each child has placed his button, enlist students' help in counting the buttons in each set. Invite students to compare the results with their predictions.

Name_____

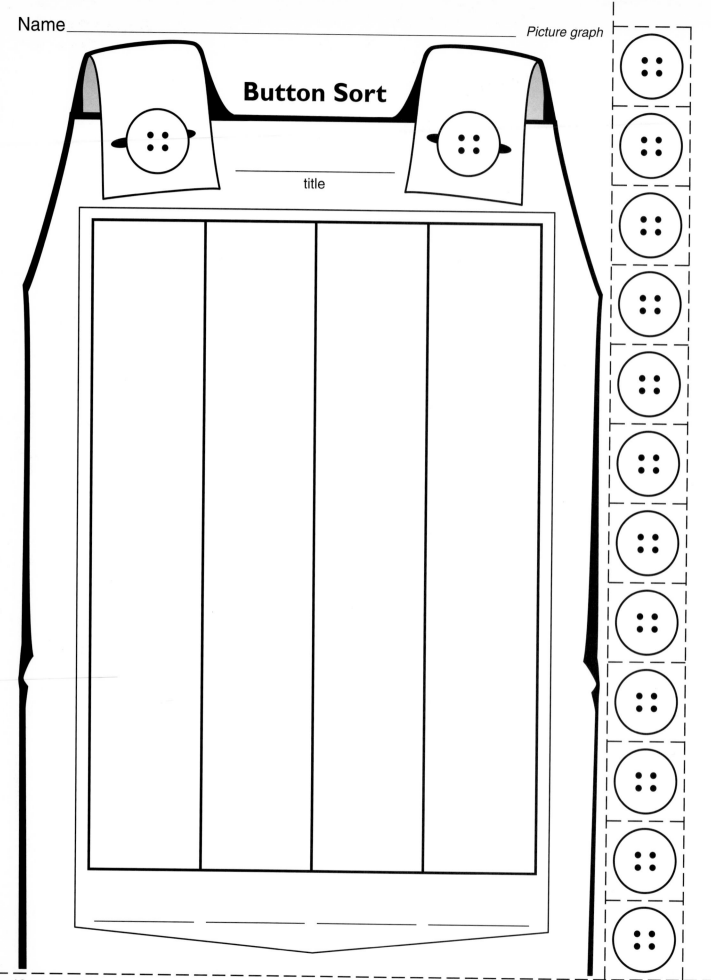

Button Sort

_____
title

Note to the teacher: Use with pages 16 and 17.

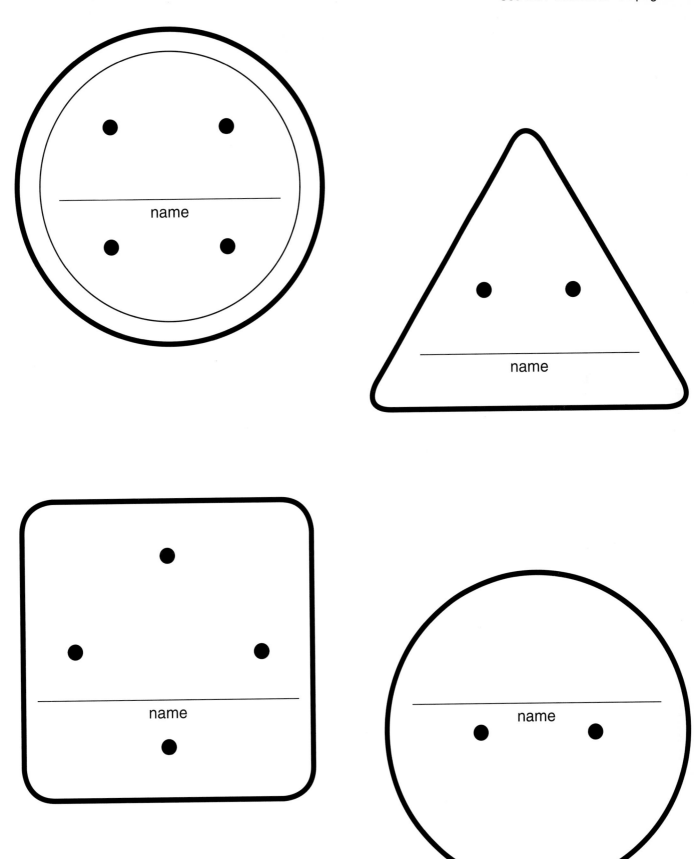

name

name

name

name

Data Crunching

Students can sink their teeth into this tasty picture graph activity!

Materials for Each Student

- programmed copy of the recording sheet on page 22 and the graph on page 23
- copy of the cracker patterns on page 22
- four different crackers
- napkin
- foam cup
- scissors
- glue

Other Materials

- five index cards
- sentence strip
- crayons
- permanent markers

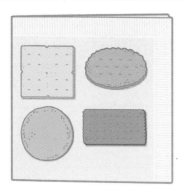

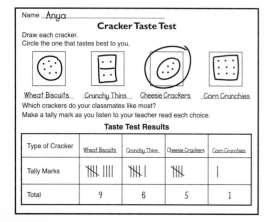

1. Introduce It!

Tempt students with some delicious data collecting by informing them that a *picture graph* represents real things using pictures, photographs, or illustrations. Then tell students that they will conduct a taste test to make a picture graph about their classmates' favorite snack crackers.

2. Collect It!

To prepare for the taste test, make one copy of the recording sheet on page 22 and one copy of the graph on page 23. Program the blank lines on both pages with the names of different crackers obtained for the taste test. Make a class set of each programmed page. Then give each student four crackers (one of each type), a napkin, and a copy of the recording sheet. To begin, show one cracker to students. Instruct each child to draw and color the cracker in the space provided and then taste some of it, leaving the rest for later tasting. Guide students through this process with the remaining cracker types. Have each student decide which cracker she prefers, tasting any crackers again as desired. Then tell her to circle her preferred cracker on the recording sheet.

Next, individually invite students to share their cracker preferences. As students share, have each child make a tally mark on the table to indicate each choice. (Remind her to make a tally mark for her own preference too.) Then have each student write the total number of tally marks for each cracker in the space provided.

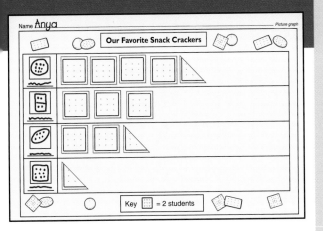

Name Anya   *Picture graph*

Our Favorite Snack Crackers

Key = 2 students

3. Display It! Discuss It!

To help each child make a picture graph of the taste-test results, give her scissors, glue, a copy of the cracker patterns on page 22, and a programmed copy of page 23. Have her draw each cracker in the corresponding box on the graph. Point out the key at the bottom of the graph, explaining that each cracker stands for two students. Further explain that a cracker pattern may be cut in half to show one student. (Suggest that students cut the patterns diagonally to ensure even cutting.)

Next, instruct each child to cut the patterns apart. Have her refer to her taste-test results and then glue the corresponding number of crackers in each row of her graph. Invite students to study the resulting graph and share their observations. Use the provided questions to guide the discussion.

Questions
Which cracker did more students prefer?
Which cracker did fewer students prefer?
If we were having a class party, which cracker would you suggest that the teacher buy? Explain why.
Look at the key. If each cracker only stood for one student, how might the graph look different? *(Possible answers: There wouldn't be any half crackers. There would be more crackers in each row.)*

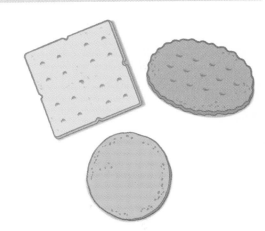

4. Extend It!

Which drink do students prefer with their favorite crackers? Find out with this easy-to-prepare display! Have students brainstorm a list of drink choices. Then take a class vote to determine the four most popular choices. Program one index card for each drink choice plus one card for "other." Program a sentence strip to read "Which drink do you prefer?" Display the resulting graph labels on a centrally located table as shown.

Next, give each child a foam cup. Have her hold the cup upside down and write her name in permanent marker on the rim. Instruct each student to stack her cup upside down on the table behind the appropriate card to indicate her drink choice in turn. After all cups have been stacked, ask students how this type of graph differs from the picture graph previously created. *(This graph uses real objects to display data, while the picture graph uses pictures to represent real things.)* Then lead a discussion about the results. Cheers!

Recording Sheet

Use with pages 20 and 21.

Name _____

Cracker Taste Test

Draw each cracker.
Circle the one that tastes best to you.

☐ ☐ ☐ ☐

_____ _____ _____ _____

Which crackers do your classmates like most?
Make a tally mark as you listen to your teacher read each choice.

Taste Test Results

Type of Cracker				
Tally Marks				
Total				

Cracker Patterns

Use with pages 20 and 21.

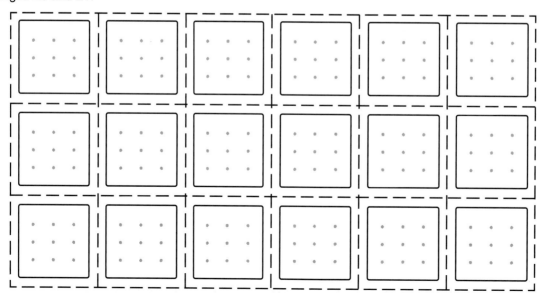

Name

Our Favorite Snack Crackers

Key ▦ = 2 students

Note to the teacher: Use with pages 20 and 21.

Picturing the Savings!

Provide plenty of picture graph practice with this cool coupon-clipping activity!

Materials

- 2 copies of page 26 for each group of 4 students
- copy of page 27 for each pair of students
- multiple-page coupon circular for each group
- grocery store circular for each pair of students (circulars from different stores)
- sheet of chart paper for each group
- marker for each group
- paper for each group
- scissors
- glue sticks

1. Introduce It!

Motivate your class to snip and clip by holding up a multiple-page coupon circular for everyone to see. Announce that students will be working together to create *picture graphs* based on the different types of coupons found in circulars such as the one being displayed. Remind students that a picture graph is a graph that uses related pictures, photographs, or illustrations to show data. Then invite students to suggest possible categories by which the coupons might be sorted, such as dairy items and frozen foods.

2. Collect It!

Divide students into groups of four. Give each group a coupon circular, scissors, several glue sticks, a sheet of chart paper, a marker, and two copies of page 26. Instruct the group to separate the circular's pages so that each student has at least one page of coupons. Direct each child to cut out all of his coupons. Have an appointed recorder title a sheet of paper for each category listed at the top of page 26. Then tell the group members to sort the coupons accordingly.

3. Display It! Discuss It!

Direct a member from each group to list down the left side of the sheet of chart paper only those categories for which coupons have been found. Remind the student to leave room at the top for a title. Then have the child draw lines to create rows as shown. Next, instruct the group members to cut apart the symbol cards on page 26. For each category, tell the group members to glue one symbol for every two coupons found in the category. Point out that a symbol may be cut in half diagonally to represent one coupon. Remind students to space the symbols apart evenly to avoid misinterpretation. Then have a group member write a title and add a key. Instruct students to discuss the resulting picture graphs. Use questions such as the following to spark the discussion: Which categories offered the most (or the fewest) coupons? Why do you think there are more (or fewer) coupons in this category? Then display the picture graphs in a prominent location and invite students to compare the results.

Aisle-by-Aisle Savings	
Cans and jars	◣
Dairy	▢ ▢ ◣
Frozen foods	▢
Beverages	▢ ▢
Breakfast items	◣
Baking items	▢ ▢
Meat	◣
Snacks and cookies	▢ ▢ ◣
Miscellaneous	▢ ▢ ▢

Key: ▢ = 2 coupons

4. Extend It!

For more picture graph practice, pair students. Give each twosome a grocery store circular and a copy of page 27. Direct the pair to search the circular for the store's weekly specials. Each time the partners find a sale item that fits one of the six categories on page 27, have them make one tally mark in the corresponding shopping cart. Then instruct each pair to create at the bottom of page 27 a picture graph based on the tallies recorded in the shopping carts. Make sure students use an appropriate symbol and include a key that explains the symbol's value. Once students are finished, have each pair share its graph with the class and point out the category that offered the greatest number of discounts.

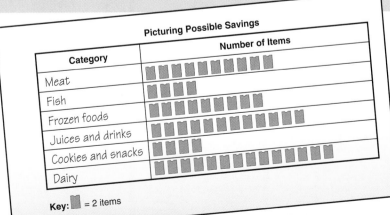

Picturing Possible Savings

Category	Number of Items
Meat	▮▮▮▮▮▮▮▮▮
Fish	▮▮▮
Frozen foods	▮▮▮▮▮▮▮▮
Juices and drinks	▮▮▮▮▮▮▮▮▮▮
Cookies and snacks	▮▮▮
Dairy	▮▮▮▮▮▮

Key: ▮ = 2 items

Coupon Categories

cans and jars

dairy

frozen foods

beverages

breakfast items

baking items

meat

snacks and cookies

deli items

cleaning and laundry supplies

personal care and medicine

miscellaneous

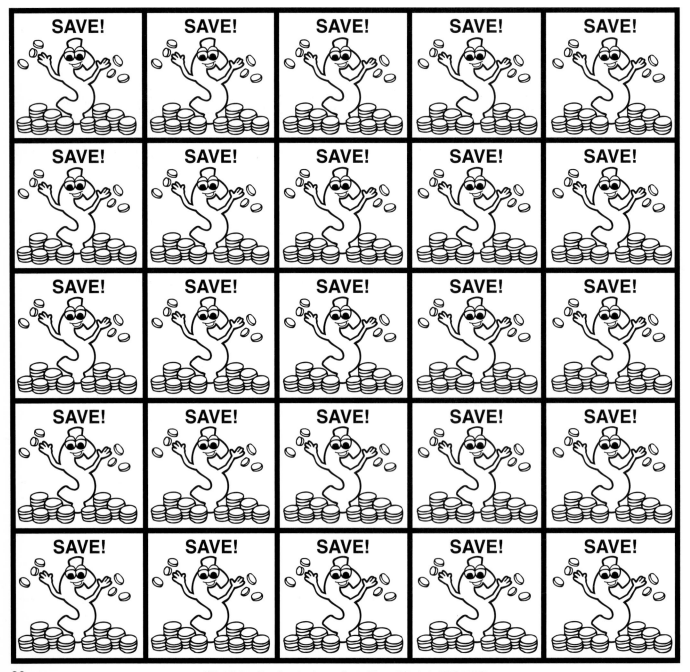

Names _____

Storewide Savings

Study the categories on the shopping carts below.
Locate items in the grocery store circular for the categories.
For each one, circle the item and make a tally mark on the matching cart.
Complete the picture graph with the results.

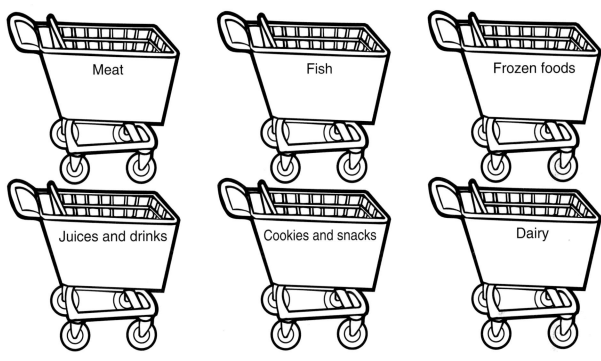

Meat	Fish	Frozen foods
Juices and drinks	Cookies and snacks	Dairy

Picturing Possible Savings

Category	Number of Items

Key: = _____ items

A Tasty Tally

Build students' data skills with this symbolic graph activity, which is good enough to eat!

Materials for Each Student
- copy of pages 30 and 31
- ¼ cup of Froot Loops cereal in a snack-size resealable plastic bag
- crayons

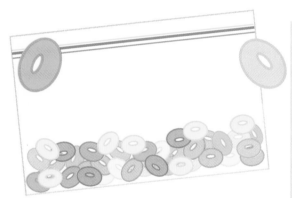

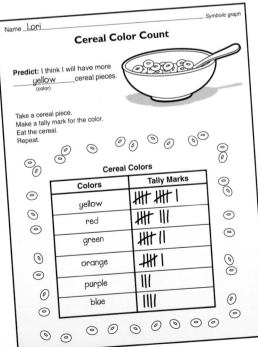

Name Lori

Symbolic graph

Cereal Color Count

Predict: I think I will have more ___yellow___ cereal pieces.
(color)

Take a cereal piece.
Make a tally mark for the color.
Eat the cereal.
Repeat.

Cereal Colors

Colors	Tally Marks
yellow	卌 卌 I
red	卌 III
green	卌 II
orange	卌 I
purple	III
blue	IIII

1. Introduce It!

Give students a spoonful of information by explaining that a *symbolic graph* is made using identical symbols, such as tally marks, to show data. Explain to students that they are going to create a symbolic graph to help them determine whether there is more of one color of Froot Loops cereal pieces than another. Further explain to students that they will use tally marks to keep track of the number of each color of cereal. Model how to draw tally marks, reminding students to mark a diagonal line across the previous four lines for every fifth tally. Then let the snacking begin!

2. Collect It! Display It!

To begin, give each student a copy of page 30 and a bag of cereal. Tell each child to list on her graph each cereal color. Then ask her to predict which color will appear most often in her bag of cereal. Have her write her prediction in the space provided.

Next, instruct her to remove a cereal piece, make a tally mark for the color, and then eat it. Have her repeat this with the remaining cereal pieces. (Allow any student who does not like the cereal to put each piece aside after she records the color, and then she can discard the cereal later.)

3. Discuss It!

After students have completed their symbolic graphs, ask them to consider why they used tally marks instead of numbers to keep track of the cereal colors. Guide students to understand that they ate each cereal piece as it was taken out of the bag; therefore, they needed to record the color of each piece one at a time. Also explain that if they used numbers, they would have had to erase the number each time they picked a cereal piece. Lead them to conclude that tally marks are better for keeping track of data that must be counted one at a time, while numbers are better for recording data that is counted all at once.

Next, ask each child to consider whether her prediction matched her results. Then use the following questions to prompt a discussion about students' findings.

Questions

Look at your graph. Which color(s) did you have the most of? Which color(s) did you have the least of?

How is your graph different from your classmates' graphs? *(Possible answers: They include different colors, they show different amounts of cereal pieces for each color, or the total number of tally marks is different.)*

From looking at the graph alone, how can you determine how many cereal pieces you ate in all? *(Count all the tally marks.)*

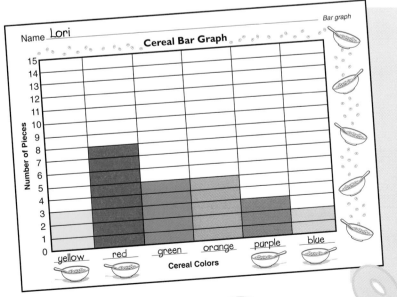

4. Extend It!

Give students another serving of graphing experience with this bar graph activity! Provide each child with a copy of page 31. Have her label the graph with the corresponding cereal colors. Then instruct her to color a space in the appropriate column for each cereal piece she ate. Direct her to place her bar graph and tally chart side by side and compare the displays. Lead students to realize that the same data appears on both graphs. Invite students to tell which type of graph they prefer and why.

Cereal Color Count

Predict: I think I will have more

_____ cereal pieces.
     (color)

Take a cereal piece.
Make a tally mark for the color.
Eat the cereal.
Repeat.

Cereal Colors

Colors	Tally Marks

Name _____

Cereal Bar Graph

15					
14					
13					
12					
11					
10					
9					
8					
7					
6					
5					
4					
3					
2					
1					
0					

Number of Pieces

Cereal Colors

Note to the teacher: Use with "Extend It!" on page 29.

31

Special Study Spots

Use this symbolic-graph activity to help students determine their favorite homework spots.

Materials
- copy of the survey sheet on page 34 for each student
- copy of the graph on page 34 for each student
- copy of page 35 for each group

Name **James**

Special Study Spot Survey

Where do you usually do your homework?
Mark an **X** to show your answer.

Kitchen **X**

Bedroom ___

Family room ___

Dining room ___

Other ___

©The Education Center, Inc. • *Gotta Have Graphs!* • TEC60780

1. Introduce It!
Begin this activity by asking your students if they've ever completed a survey. Have several students share their experiences. Next, explain that today they're going to complete a survey about where they do their homework. Then explain that they will use the survey data to help them create a *symbolic graph.* Tell students that a symbolic graph uses a symbol such as a tally mark to represent data.

2. Collect It!
Give each student a copy of one survey from the top of page 34. Ask him to think about where he usually completes his homework and mark an X on the appropriate line. (Clarify that if a child goes to afterschool care or a caretaker's home after school, he should indicate the room there in which he completes his homework.) Collect the completed surveys.

3. Display It! Discuss It!

Next, provide each student with a copy of the graph on the bottom of page 34. As you read aloud each survey response, instruct each student to make a tally mark in the corresponding row to record his classmate's answer. Pause after every few surveys and have students predict in which location they think most students do their homework. After sharing all the survey results, have students review the data on their resulting symbolic graphs. Invite volunteers to share if their predictions were correct, or if they were surprised by the results.

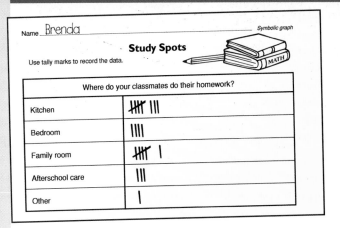

4. Extend It!

Challenge students to discover more about their classmates' homework habits by making bar graphs! Divide the class into four groups. Give each group a copy of page 35 and assign each group a different homework-related question from the list shown. Instruct a recorder in each group to write the assigned question in the space provided. Have the group members discuss possible responses and write them in the first column as shown. (Remind students to include an all-inclusive response such as "other" or "none of the above.") Next, instruct each group member to use his pencil to shade a space that indicates his response. Then have each group switch graphs with another group. Direct each student to indicate his response to the new question by shading the appropriate box on the grid. Continue the activity until all students have responded to each group's question. Return the graphs to the original group. Then have each group discuss the results and share the findings with the class. Ask students what they learned about their classmates' homework habits as a result of the study.

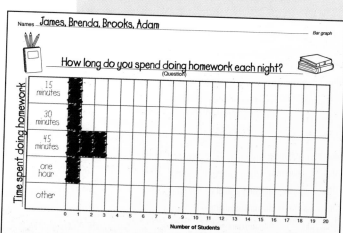

Homework-Related Questions

For which subject do you prefer doing homework?
When do you usually do your homework?
How long do you spend doing homework each night?
Who helps you do your homework?

Name _____

Special Study Spot Survey

Where do you usually do your homework?

Mark an **X** to show your answer.

Kitchen ____

Bedroom ____

Family room ____

Dining room ____

Other ____

Name _____

Special Study Spot Survey

Where do you usually do your homework?

Mark an **X** to show your answer.

Kitchen ____

Bedroom ____

Family room ____

Dining room ____

Other ____

Name _____   *Symbolic graph*

Study Spots

Use tally marks to record the data.

Where do your classmates do their homework?	
Kitchen	
Bedroom	
Family room	
Afterschool care	
Other	

Note to the teacher: Use with pages 32 and 33.

Names _____

Bar graph

(Question) _____

	0	1	2	3	4	5	6	7	8	9	10	11	12	13	14	15	16	17	18	19	20

Number of Students

©The Education Center, Inc. • *Gotta Have Graphs!* • TEC60780

Note to the teacher: Use with "Extend It!" on page 33.

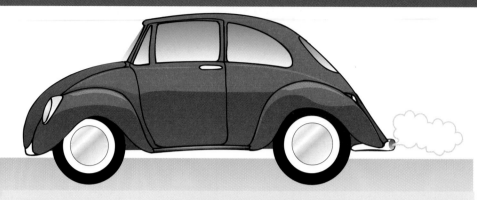

Rev It Up!

Expect high performance when students construct symbolic graphs about car advertisements!

Materials

- copy of pages 38 and 39 for each student
- discarded magazines
- sheet of poster board per group
- ruler per group
- construction paper scraps
- glue
- markers
- scissors

1. Introduce It!

Supercharge students' graphing skills! To begin, ask students to brainstorm ways to classify cars, such as sports cars, economy cars, luxury cars, and sport-utility vehicles. Then have students predict which type is most advertised most frequently advertised in the magazines and why. Explain to students that they will construct *symbolic graphs* (graphs that use symbols to represent data) to show the number of advertisements for each type of car.

2. Collect It! Display It!

To begin the data collection, provide each child with a copy of page 38. Point out the car types indicated on the table. Have each student record her prediction for which car type is most frequently advertised in magazines. Then divide students into small groups. Give each group several magazines. Direct each group member to locate as many car advertisements as she can find. As she encounters each one, tell her to show the advertisement to her group. Then have the group identify the car's type. Direct each group member to make a tally mark for the car in the corresponding space on her copy of page 38. Then, to prevent her from recording the same data more than once, have her fold the corner of the advertisement page.

To compile the results, use an overhead projector to display a transparency copy of page 38. Ask an appointed reporter from each group to announce to the class how many advertisements her group found for each car type. Record the corresponding number of tally marks on the transparency. At the same time, have each student from the remaining groups record the tally marks on her table, adding them to any previously written marks.

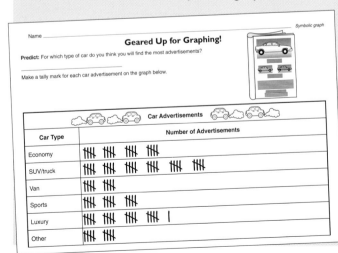

3. Discuss It!

Use the provided questions as appropriate to prompt a discussion with students about their completed graphs.

I was surprised by the number of luxury car ads I found!

Questions

Which type of car was advertised most frequently? Least frequently?

For which types of cars did you find about the same number of advertisements?

If the "SUV/truck" category were divided into two separate categories, how might the data differ? How might it stay the same?

Why do you think certain types of cars are advertised more frequently than other types?

4. Extend It!

Survey students to learn about their automotive preferences! Provide each student with a copy of page 39. Read each question aloud. Instruct each child to raise her hand when you read her preference. Tell each child to count the raised hands for each preference and record the total on her copy of the table. Next, divide students into six groups. Give each group a ruler, a sheet of poster board, and access to construction paper scraps in one color. Tell the group to construct a symbolic graph for an assigned survey question. Have the group members first agree on a symbol for the data, as well as the number of students the symbol represents. Then instruct the group to cut out a sufficient number of the symbol (using fractional parts of the symbol as needed) plus one more for the key, prepare the graph, and glue the symbols in place. Invite groups to share their graphs with the class. For further discussion, prompt students to speculate how the results might differ if they conducted the survey among adults.

Minimum Driving Age

Age	Number of Students
16 years old	●●●◗
18 years old	●◗
21 years old	◗
Key: ● = 4 students	

Symbolic graph

Geared Up for Graphing!

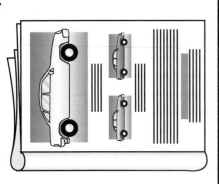

Predict: For which type of car do you think you will find the most advertisements?

_____

Make a tally mark for each car advertisement on the graph below.

Car Advertisements

Number of Advertisements

Car Type					
Economy					
SUV/truck					
Van					
Sports					
Luxury					
Other					

Note to the teacher: Use with pages 36 and 37.

On the Road

1. Which is your favorite type of car?

Car Type	Number of Responses
Economy	
SUV/truck	
Van	
Sports	
Luxury	
Other	
Total	

2. Which color car do you prefer?

Color	Number of Responses
Black	
Blue	
Red	
Silver	
Gold	
Other	
Total	

3. Which number of car doors do you prefer?

Number of Doors	Number of Responses
Two doors	
Four doors	
Total	

4. Which do you prefer to listen to while riding in the car?

Listening Preference	Number of Responses
Radio	
Tape or CD	
Nothing	
Other	
Total	

5. Which is the best minimum driving age?

Age	Number of Responses
16 years old	
18 years old	
21 years old	
Total	

6. Which is the best state highway speed limit?

Speed Limit	Number of Responses
55 mph	
60 mph	
65 mph	
Total	

Note to the teacher: Use with "Extend It!" on page 37.

Plotting Pockets

Students will have line plots in their back pockets after digging into this investigation!

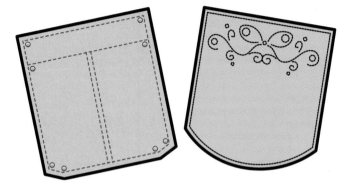

Materials for Each Student

- copy of pages 42 and 43
- sticky note

1. Introduce It!

Sew up understanding about *line plots* by having students graph how many pockets they have! Begin by explaining that a line plot uses Xs to tell how many pieces of data there are for each number. The plot shows whether data is all bunched up or spread out. Then inform your students that they will create a line plot to determine how many pockets are in the classroom.

2. Collect It!

As a class, establish guidelines for counting pockets. For example, have the class decide whether a student should count jacket pockets, shirt pockets, or smaller pockets within larger pockets. List the guidelines on the board. Then give each child a copy of page 42. Ask him to count the pockets on his clothing and write the total in the space provided on his paper. Next, to help students complete the table, announce the first number on the table and tell students who have that many pockets to stand. Enlist your seated students' help in counting their standing classmates. Tell the standing students to sit down; then have all the students write the total in the appropriate box on the table. Continue in this same manner for the remaining numbers on the table.

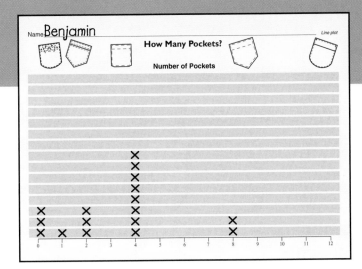

Name Benjamin

Line plot

How Many Pockets?

Number of Pockets

Questions

What is the greatest number of pockets any student has?
What is the least number of pockets any student has?
How many students have [the greatest number] pockets?
How many students have [the least number] pockets?
How many pockets do most students have? How many pockets do the least students have?

3. Display It! Discuss It!

After students record the pocket data, give each child a copy of page 43, and inform him that he will need his completed table from page 42 as well. Tell the child to locate on the table the number of students that have zero pockets. Then have him locate the zero on his line plot. Beginning at the bottom, instruct the student to mark the corresponding number of Xs to show how many students have zero pockets, stacking the Xs vertically above the zero. (Advise him to use the gray bars to help him space the Xs.) To complete the line plot, direct youngsters to repeat this process for the remaining numbers of pockets. After students complete their plots, use the provided questions to prompt a discussion about the results.

4. Extend It!

So what's in your pocket? This fun activity will help students see the similarity of their pocket contents. Have each student pull out one item from one of his pockets and place it in front of him. Next, have each student show his item to the class as you record the name of the item at the bottom of the board as shown. *(Record each item only once.)* Then give each child a sticky note and instruct him to write his name on it. Next, direct each child, in turn, to go to the board and place his sticky note directly above the name of the item he had in his pocket. After each child has posted his sticky note, have students observe and discuss the resulting data. Did each item only have a few sticky notes, or did some items have several sticky notes? Have students explain why some items may have been more popular than others. Ask students to help you title the graph.

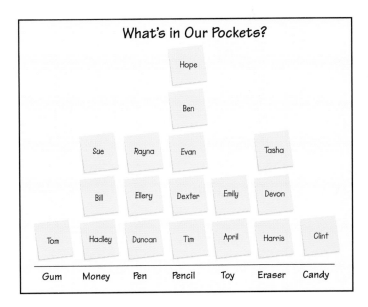

What's in Our Pockets?

Name _____   *Line plot*

Class Pocket Count

1. How many pockets do you have?

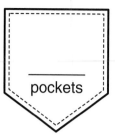

_____
pockets

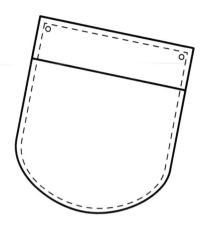

2. How many pockets do all the students have?

Number of Pockets	Number of Students
0 pockets	
1 pocket	
2 pockets	
3 pockets	
4 pockets	
5 pockets	
6 pockets	
7 pockets	
8 pockets	
9 pockets	
10 pockets	
11 pockets	
12 pockets	

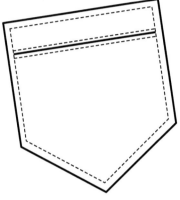

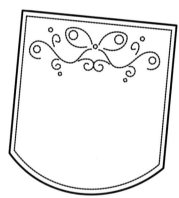

Note to the teacher: Use with pages 40 and 41.

Name _____

How Many Pockets?

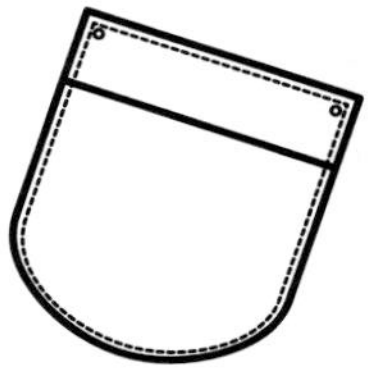

Number of Pockets

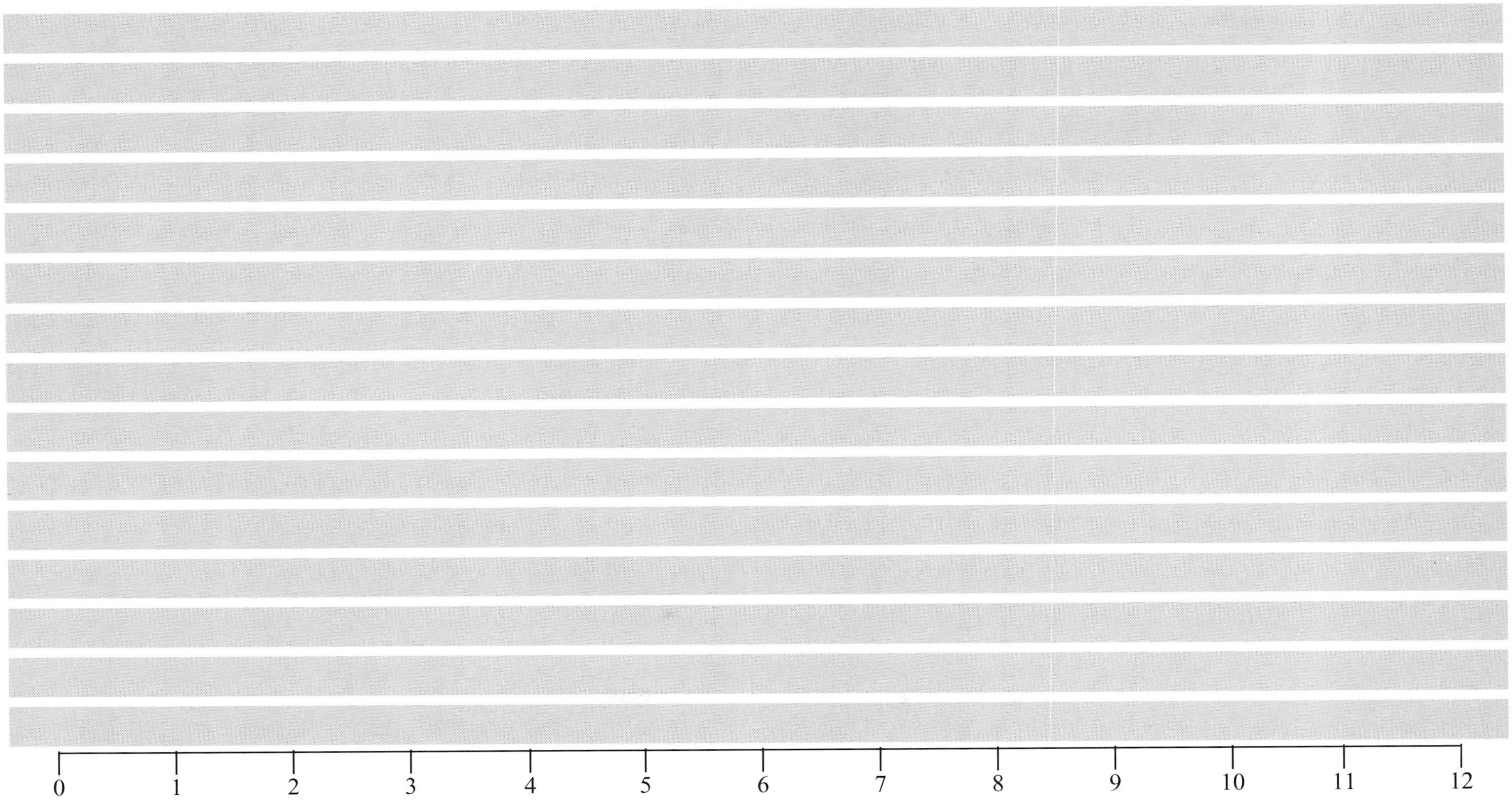

0	1	2	3	4	5	6	7	8	9	10	11	12

©The Education Center, Inc. • *Gotta Have Graphs!* • TEC60780

Note to the teacher: Use with pages 40 and 41.

43

A Slice of Summer

Whet your students' appetites for graphing with this activity that's just "ripe" for teaching line plots!

Materials for Each Student

- copy of pages 46 and 47
- one-inch watermelon slice (similar to the one shown)
- toothpick
- napkin
- sticky note
- marker

1. Introduce It!

Serve up a slice of graphing information by telling students that *line plots* are used to show whether data is all spread out or bunched up together. Inform students that they will be constructing a line plot to show the number of seeds in a slice of watermelon.

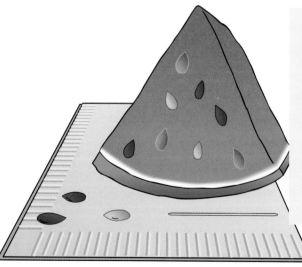

2. Collect It!

Give each student a watermelon slice, a toothpick, a napkin, a sticky note, and a marker. Have the student use the toothpick to remove each seed from her slice. (Invite students to eat their watermelon as they do so.) When all the seeds have been removed, instruct each student to count her seeds. Then have her use the marker and the provided sticky note to record her seed total. Have each student set her seeds aside for a later activity.

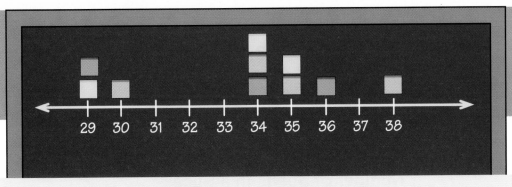

3. Display It! Discuss It!

To analyze the results, determine from students the fewest number of seeds per slice and the greatest number of seeds per slice. Then draw a number line on the board and label it so that it begins and ends with those numbers. Have each student, in turn, attach her sticky note above the corresponding number on the line.

Next, give each child a copy of page 46. Instruct the student to complete the line plot using the data from the board. Have her answer the follow-up questions on the page. Conclude the activity by leading students in a discussion about the line plot's results. Use the provided questions below to prompt discussion.

Questions

What might cause a wide range in the number of seeds per slice? *(Possible answers: The number of seeds may depend on which part of the watermelon the slice came from; some slices may have been larger than others.)*

Why might the results differ if a different watermelon was used? *(Possible answer: The size of the watermelon probably affects its number of seeds.)*

How might the line plot change if the slices were smaller? *(The numbers on the plot and the range might be smaller.)* Bigger? *(The numbers on the plot and the range might be larger.)*

Watermelon Seeds

Key: ⬭ = 2 seeds

Type of Seed	Number of Seeds
Dark	◊ ◊ ◊ ◊ ◊ ◊ ◊ ◊ ◊ ◊ ◊ ◊
Light	◊ ◊

4. Extend It!

Any way you slice it, this picture graph activity is sure to be the pick of the patch! Give each student a copy of page 47. Instruct each child to sort her seeds into two categories—dark and light. Direct her to record the totals in the space provided. Have her determine how many seeds each seed picture will represent and write it in the provided key. Then instruct her to complete the picture graph. Finally, have her interpret her graph by writing two statements about the results. Invite students to share their findings. Now that's the way to sweeten students' understanding of picture graphs!

Plotting the Patch

Study the data on the board.

For each sticky note, mark an X above the matching number on
    the line plot below.

Then use the line plot to complete the items that follow.

Number of Seeds in a Slice

1. What was the least number of seeds found in a slice?
    _____ The most? _____

2. How many seeds did most students find? _____

3. Think about the number of seeds you found. Did you
    find fewer seeds or more seeds than most of your
    classmates? _____

Simply Seeds

How many of each type of seed are in your watermelon slice? Follow the steps below to find out!

Sort your watermelon seeds.
Write the number of seeds in the box.

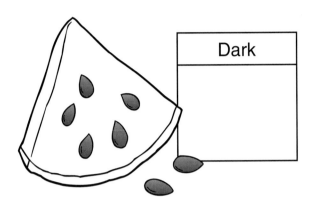
Dark

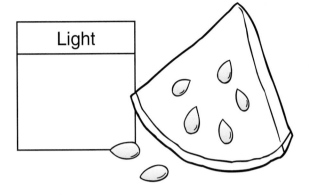
Light

Use the results to create a picture graph.

Watermelon Seeds	
Key: ☐ = _____ seeds	
Type of Seed	**Number of Seeds**
Dark	
Light	

Study your graph. Write 2 statements about the results.

1. _____

_____

2. _____

_____

Beboppin' Line Plots

Jazz up data analysis with these lyrical line plots!

Materials
- copy of pages 50 and 51 for each student
- music CD insert for each pair (should be appropriate for classroom use and contain several song titles and song lengths)

One Cool Cat
1. Steel Beat 2:47
2. Sutton Swing 3:03
3. Chevy Hop 7:00
4. Bruce's Bee Bop 4:16
5. Blue-Eye Groove 3:20
6. Jumpin' Jetta 5:00

1. Introduce It!
Help students get into the swing of analyzing data when they investigate song lengths! To begin, give each student a copy of page 50. Invite students to think about recorded songs they have heard. Ask each child to predict the average time length of a song. Have him write his prediction in the space provided at the top of page 50. Then tell students that they will find the average song length on a CD. Further explain that each student will display the times on a *line plot,* a number line that shows variations in data.

2. Collect It!
To get youngsters started in collecting the data, pair students and give each twosome a CD insert. Direct the pair to open the insert and locate the song length for each song title. Have each partner list on page 50 up to 12 song lengths that are less than eight minutes long. Then tell him to round each one to the nearest half minute.

3. Display It! Discuss It!

Guide students to display each CD's song lengths on a line plot. To begin, point out to youngsters the line plot on page 50. For each rounded time, direct each child to mark an X on a gray bar above the corresponding time.

Next, lead students to analyze the data by identifying the *range, median, mode,* and *outliers.* Use the information in the box on the right to help youngsters compute the statistics. Have each child record his answers at the bottom of page 50. Then explain to students that a median is a type of average. Ask each child to compare his data's median to his prediction. Have him record his thoughts in the space provided. Invite students to share their results and observations with the class.

Range	— Find the difference between the longest and shortest times.
Median	— Find the time that falls in the middle. If the number of times is odd, the median is the time directly in the middle. If the number of times is even, find the time that falls halfway in between.
Mode	— Find the time or times that occur most frequently.
Outliers	— Find any times that are much larger or smaller than the rest of the data.

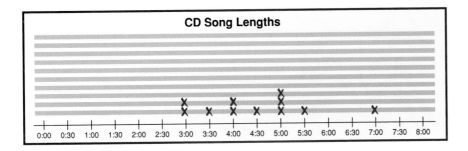

CD Song Lengths

0:00 0:30 1:00 1:30 2:00 2:30 3:00 3:30 4:00 4:30 5:00 5:30 6:00 6:30 7:00 7:30 8:00

4. Extend It!

Lead students to investigate the average number of songs on a CD! Collect the CD inserts and redistribute them to student pairs. Also give each child a copy of page 51. Tell each student to determine the number of tracks listed on the CD insert. Then have him plot this data on the line plot. Direct pairs to rotate the inserts until each child has plotted each CD's number of tracks. Then tell each student to title his line plot and complete the page.

Tuning In to Song Lengths

On average, how long is a song? Follow the directions below to find out!

Directions: Think about the recorded songs you have heard. Predict the average time length for a song. Write your prediction to the nearest half minute.

Prediction: _____ minutes

Write the title of the CD in the space provided. Then list each song length (that is less than eight minutes long). Round each time to the nearest half minute. For each rounded time, mark an X on the line plot above the corresponding time. (Remember to start at the bottom.)

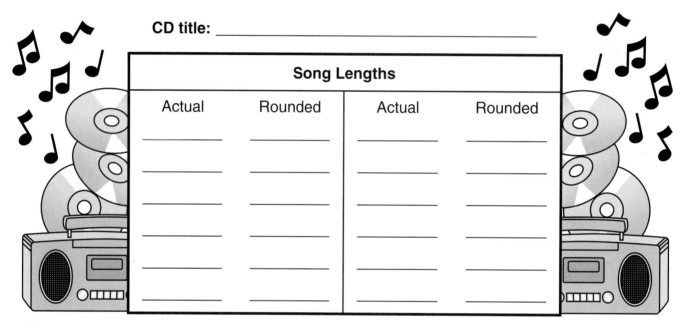

CD title: _____

Song Lengths			
Actual	Rounded	Actual	Rounded
_____	_____	_____	_____
_____	_____	_____	_____
_____	_____	_____	_____
_____	_____	_____	_____
_____	_____	_____	_____
_____	_____	_____	_____

CD Song Lengths

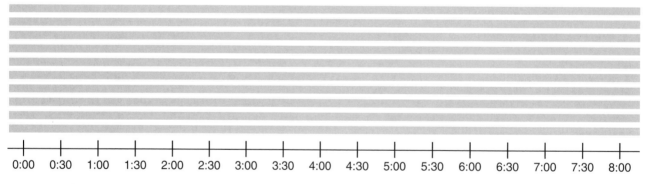

0:00 0:30 1:00 1:30 2:00 2:30 3:00 3:30 4:00 4:30 5:00 5:30 6:00 6:30 7:00 7:30 8:00

Use the data shown on the line plot to complete each item below.

1. Range = _____
2. Median = _____
3. Mode or modes (if any) = _____
4. Outlier or outliers (if any) = _____
5. Write a statement that compares your prediction to the median song length.

_____

_____

Tracking CD Data

Study the CD insert. Determine the total number of tracks. Plot an X above the corresponding number. Repeat this process with each remaining insert. Then write a title.

_____
(title)

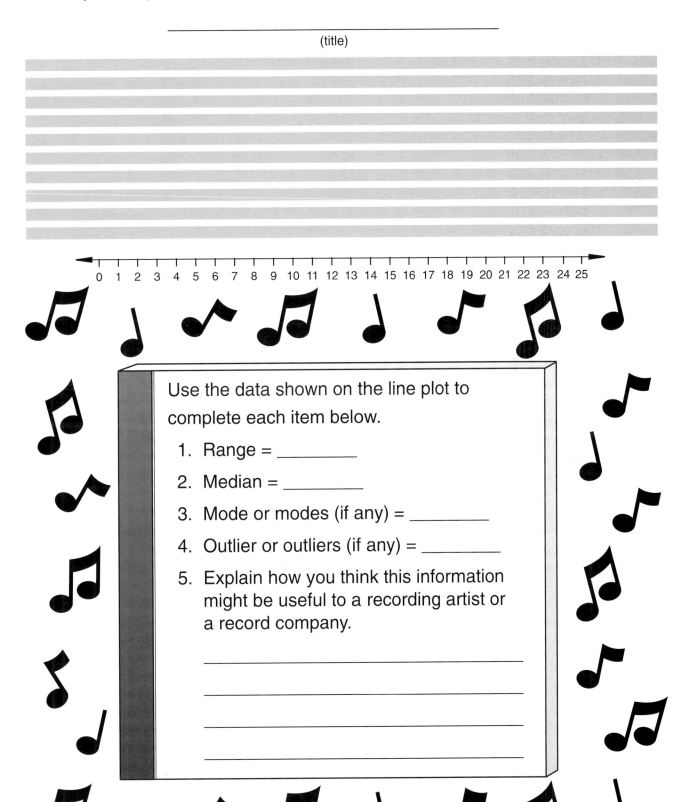

Use the data shown on the line plot to complete each item below.

1. Range = _____

2. Median = _____

3. Mode or modes (if any) = _____

4. Outlier or outliers (if any) = _____

5. Explain how you think this information might be useful to a recording artist or a record company.

_____

_____

_____

_____

Bakery Business

Tempt students' taste buds with this mouthwatering lesson on bar graphs!

Activity #13

Materials for Each Student
- copy of pages 54 and 55
- crayons

1. Introduce It!

Use this tasty graphing activity to find out your students' preferences for bakery items. To begin, explain that a *bar graph* uses bars to compare information from several categories. Tell students that they will be creating bar graphs based on what they would choose at a bakery.

Bakery Items	Tally Marks	Total
Muffin	III	3
Pie	I	1
Cake	⊬⊬⊬ I	6
Cookie	⊬⊬⊬ III	8
Doughnut	III	3

2. Collect It!

To collect the information, take your students on an imaginary trip to the bakery! Draw a tally table on the board and label it as shown. Tell students that the bakery features five items: muffins, pies, cakes, cookies, and doughnuts. Then have each student make a tally mark on the table to indicate her choice at the bakery. With students' help, write the total number of tally marks for each item.

3. Display It! Discuss It!

Direct students to study the tally table on the board. Give each student a copy of page 54 and have her color the bar graph to display the information. Use the results to prompt a discussion about students' bakery preferences. Then lead them to consider how the bar graph might be used to buy treats for a class party. *(Possible answer: They might buy more of the most preferred items.)* Ask students how the graph might look different if there were fewer choices *(the bars might be taller)* or more choices *(the bars might be shorter).*

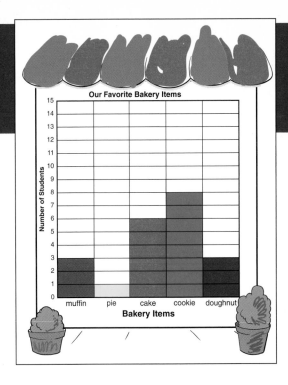

4. Extend It!

Add a little spice to graphing data! Give each student a copy of page 55. On the provided line, have the child list a selected bakery item from the previous graph. Then, on the table and the graph, ask her to list three varieties of the item (such as chocolate chip, peanut butter, and oatmeal for cookie varieties). Tell her to lay her paper and pencil on her desk. Next, direct each student to walk along an established classroom path to visit another classmate's desk. Have her mark her bakery preference on the tally table. Then, on a predetermined signal, have students move to the next desk on the path. Continue in this manner for nine additional turns. Then have students return to their seats and study the results on their tables. Direct each child to total the tally marks for each kind of bakery item and then graph the results. Pair students; then have them share their findings. Read the provided questions aloud and have pairs discuss the answers.

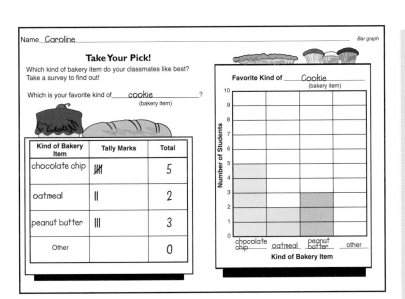

Questions

How are the graphs different? How are they alike?
Which kind of [bakery item] do most of the students surveyed prefer? The least students?
Do most of the students surveyed prefer the same kind of [bakery item] you prefer?
Why was "Other" included as one of the choices?

Bakery Bests

Our Favorite Bakery Items

Number of Students	muffin	pie	cake	cookie	doughnut
15					
14					
13					
12					
11					
10					
9					
8					
7					
6					
5					
4					
3					
2					
1					
0					

Bakery Items

Name _____

Take Your Pick!

Which kind of bakery item do your classmates like best?
Take a survey to find out!

Which is your favorite kind of _____ ?
(bakery item)

Kind of Bakery Item	Tally Marks	Total
Other		

Favorite Kind of _____
(bakery item)

Number of Students

10				
9				
8				
7				
6				
5				
4				
3				
2				
1				
0				other

Kind of Bakery Item

Note to the teacher: Use with "Extend It!" on page 53.

55

A Special Invitation

With whom would your students enjoy having lunch? Find out with this tasty bar graph activity!

Materials for Each Student

- copy of pages 58 and 59
- scissors
- two different colored crayons

Category	Number of Votes
Athlete	
Actor	
Scientist	
Musician	
Family member	
Other	

1. Introduce It!

To begin, inform students that a *bar graph* shows data using vertical or horizontal parallel bars. Each bar represents a different category. The length or height of each bar shows the number of responses for that category. Tell students that they will be creating bar graphs that show their responses to the following question: If you could have lunch with anyone, who would it be?

2. Collect It!

Draw and label a table on the board similar to the one shown. Give each student a copy of page 58. Instruct him to cut along the dotted line and set aside the top portion of the page. Next, ask him to answer the three survey questions at the bottom of the page. To tabulate the votes for the third question, announce each category, ask students who chose it to raise their hands, and write the totals on the table. Collect the surveys and set aside for later use.

3. Display It! Discuss It!

Direct students' attention to the blank graph on their copies of page 58. Point out that the number of students is represented in increments of two. Explain that each line counts as two students and that one vote may be shown by coloring halfway to a line. Also point out that the categories are shown along the bottom of the graph. To complete the graph, have each student draw and color a bar above each category to represent its total number of votes. Afterward, use the questions shown to facilitate a discussion about the results. If desired, allow time for each student to share whom he chose to have lunch with and why.

Questions
Which category had the most votes?
Which category had the fewest votes?
How does displaying the results on the bar graph instead of the surveys help readers understand the data? *(All the data is displayed in one place instead of on separate pages.)*
Why might it be difficult to display the results from question 2? *(Possible answer: There would be too many different responses.)*

4. Extend It!

Your students will be seeing double after completing this graphing activity! Begin by explaining that a double-bar graph uses a second bar to display more detailed data about each category. Tell students that they will be creating double-bar graphs that separate the girls' votes from the boys' votes. Sort the completed surveys from page 58 by gender. List the total votes for boys and girls for each category in two separate tables on the board. Then give each student a copy of page 59 and two different-colored crayons. For each category, have him draw and color a bar for the boys in one color and a bar for the girls in another color. Direct him to color the key at the bottom of the page accordingly. Lead students in a discussion about the results using questions such as the following: Did the girls vote differently than the boys? Is a single- or double-bar graph easier to interpret? Why? Wow! Double-bar graphs are double the fun!

Double-bar graph

Name

Graphing on the Double

Make a two-bar graph using different colored crayons.
One bar will show the girls' votes.
One bar will show the boys' votes.
Color the key to match.

Lunch Guests Boys and Girls Chose

Number of students

20
18
16
14
12
10
8
6
4
2
0

athlete   actor   scientist   musician   family member   other

Categories

Key Girls' votes = ☐ Boys' votes = ☐

Name_____

Be My Guest!

Use the information from the class survey to create a bar graph.

Hmmm?

Favorite Lunch Guests

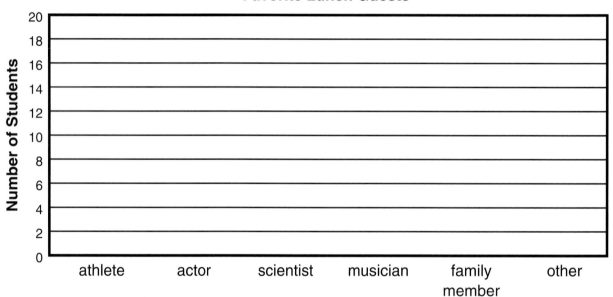

Categories

Survey

1. Are you a boy or a girl? _____

2. If you could have lunch with anyone, who would it be?

   _____

3. Circle the category that best fits this person.

   Athlete   Actor   Scientist   Musician   Family   Other
                                                                 Member

Name _____

Graphing on the Double

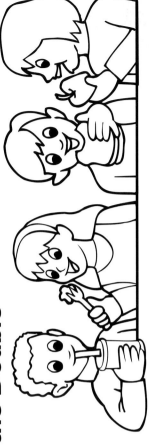

Make a double-bar graph using different-colored crayons.
One bar will show the girls' votes.
One bar will show the boys' votes.
Color the key to match.

Favorite Lunch Guests

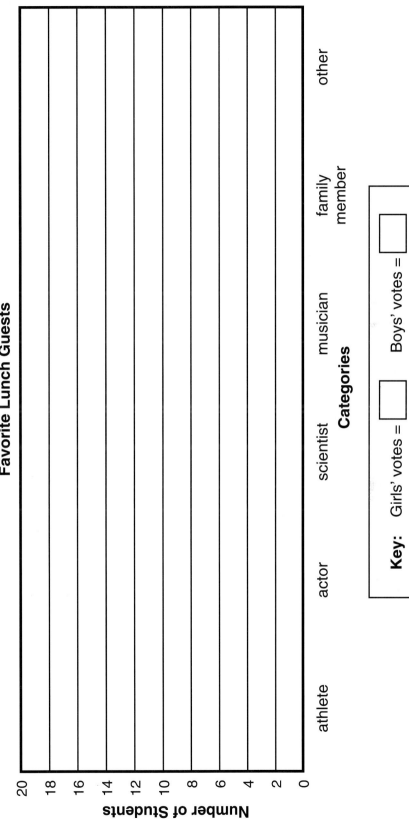

Number of Students

20
18
16
14
12
10
8
6
4
2
0

athlete   actor   scientist   musician   family   other
                                              member

Categories

Key: Girls' votes = ☐   Boys' votes = ☐

©The Education Center, Inc. • *Gotta Have Graphs!* • TEC60780

Note to the teacher: Use with "Extend It!" on page 57.

Grab Bag Graphing

This double-bar graph activity will surely grab students' interest!

Materials

- copy of pages 62 and 63 for each student
- 40 pom-poms (about 1" in diameter)
- paper lunch bag
- colored pencils

1. Introduce It!

Begin this activity by asking students to consider whether a person's dominant hand (the hand she writes with) can grab more objects than the other hand or whether there is no difference. Then tell them that they will construct *double-bar graphs* to compare the number of pom-poms each student can hold with each hand. Explain that a double-bar graph uses pairs of bars and a key to compare two sets of data.

2. Collect It!

To prepare for this hands-on investigation, place 40 pom-poms in a paper lunch bag. Place the bag at a table along with pencils and student copies of page 62. To ensure that students collect reliable data, model the appropriate way to grab pom-poms from the bag. To do this, hold up the bag by the top edge so that the bottom is not supported by any surface. Reach one hand into the bag and grab as many pom-poms as you can without supporting the bottom of the bag. Place the pom-poms on a flat surface, returning to the bag any pom-poms that dropped from your grasp. Count the pom-poms; then return them to the bag. Stress to students the importance of following this same procedure to collect the data.

Next, arrange for students to visit the center in pairs. Instruct Partner 1 to take a copy of the recording sheet (page 62). Have her follow the directions on the page. Then instruct Partner 2 to complete the activity. Tell students to leave their recording sheets at the center for later use. After every student has had a turn, return each child's recording sheet. Divide students into groups of no more than six members. Instruct each student to write her group members' pom-pom data on her recording sheet. Then tell her to indicate the best results for each group member by circling the largest number of pom-poms the student grabbed with her left hand and then her right hand.

3. Display It! Discuss It!

Help students make sense of their data by leading them to construct double-bar graphs. Give each student a copy of page 63. Instruct the student to color the first two boxes on the key (each a different color) and then number the grid appropriately for the data she collected. Have the student write each group member's name at the bottom of the page, beginning with her own name. Tell her to draw and color a vertical bar above her name to show the greatest number of pom-poms she grabbed with her left hand. Direct her to do the same for the number of pom-poms she grabbed with her right hand. Then instruct her to draw dots or stripes on both bars to indicate whether she is left-handed or right-handed. Have her repeat this process to show each group member's results and dominant hand.

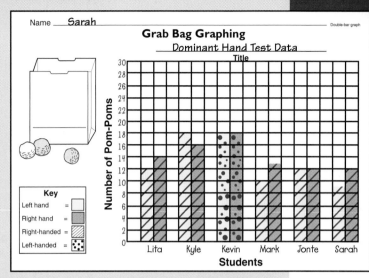

Next, ask the students in each group to study their graphs. Tell them to determine which student grabbed the most pom-poms with her right hand and which grabbed the most with her left hand. Have students discuss whether each child tended to grab more pom-poms with her dominant hand. Ask students to compare the bars and think about the differences or lack of differences. Invite them to share their conclusions.

| | Left-Handed Students Total = | | Right-Handed Students Total = | |
| | Number of Pom-Poms | | Number of Pom-Poms | |
	Left Hand	Right Hand	Left Hand	Right Hand
Group 1				
Group 2				
Group 3				
Group 4				
Total				
Mean				

4. Extend It!

After students have drawn conclusions based on the group graphs, lead them to compare data for all the students in the class. On the board, draw a table similar to the one shown, adapting it for the number of groups. As a class, determine the number of left-handed and right-handed students. Record the totals in the spaces provided. Have each group refer to its graph and total the number of pom-poms that left-handed group members grabbed with their left hands and then with their right hands. Have each group do the same for right-handed members. Ask a representative from each group to record the totals on the table. With students' input, add each column of numbers and calculate the mean. Guide students to compare the class results with the group results and revise or confirm their previous conclusions.

Handling Data

Can right-handed people grab more objects with their right hands? Can left-handed people grab more objects with their left hands? Follow the directions to find out!

Directions:

1. Write your name in the table below.
2. Check one of the boxes to show whether you are right-handed or left-handed.
3. Grab as many pom-poms as you can with your left hand. Lay them down on a flat surface. Return any pom-poms you dropped to the bag.
4. Count the pom-poms. Have your partner write the total in the table.
5. Repeat Steps 3 and 4 with your right hand.
6. Repeat Steps 3 through 5 two more times.

Student Names	Check one.		Number of Pom-Poms					
			Trial 1		Trial 2		Trial 3	
	Left-Handed	Right-Handed	Left Hand	Right Hand	Left Hand	Right Hand	Left Hand	Right Hand

Note to the teacher: Use with pages 60 and 61.

Name _____

Grab Bag Graphing

Title

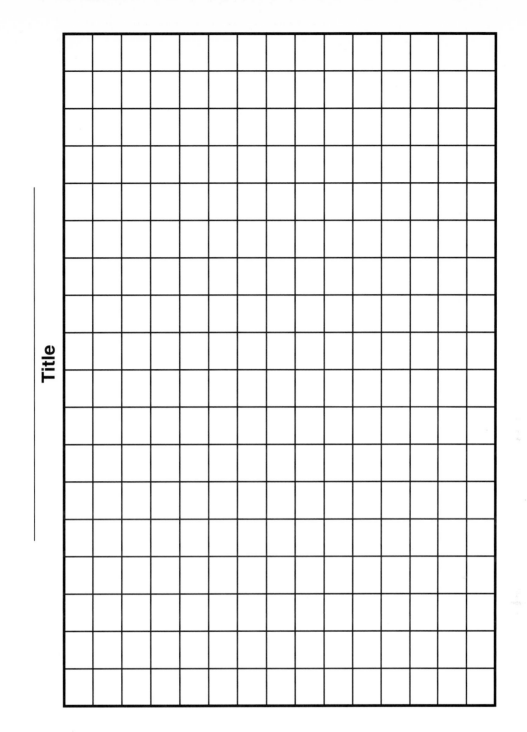

Number of Pom-Poms

Students

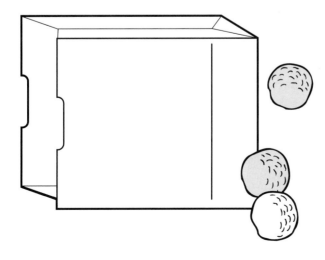

Key		
Left hand	=	☐
Right hand	=	☐
Right-handed	=	▨
Left-handed	=	▨

63

Note to the teacher: Use with pages 60 and 61.

Tracking TV Time

Make students aware of how much TV they watch with a graphing activity that puts it on the line!

Materials

- copy of pages 66 and 67 for each student
- red colored pencil for each group
- blue colored pencil for each group
- rulers for each student
- calculators

1. Introduce It!

Tune students in to this activity by asking them to predict whether they watch more than 30 hours of television each week. After listening to students' responses, explain that a *line graph* shows how data changes over time. Then announce that each student is going to create a line graph that shows the amount of television he watches outside of school each day for a week.

2. Collect It!

To begin, give each child a copy of the TV watching journal on page 66. Explain that the journal is for recording the actual times spent each day watching television. Read aloud the table's headings and answer any questions students have about where and how to record the information. (Tell each child to use the back of the page if he needs more space.) To review how to calculate elapsed time, list on the board several examples of beginning and ending times. With students' input, find the elapsed time for each example. Then have each child complete the recording sheet at home and return it by a designated day.

3:30 P.M. to 4:00 P.M. = 30 minutes

7:00 P.M. to 8:00 P.M. = 1 hour

3. Display It! Discuss It!

Once the recording sheets have been returned, check students' calculations for accuracy. Then give each student a copy of the blank graph at the bottom of page 66. Guide each child to use his data to construct a line graph. Have him complete the graph's title and then number the vertical axis to allow for the greatest number of hours he watched in one day. Then tell him to plot a point for each day's data and use a ruler to connect the points. Invite students to discuss the hours of television watched each night, identify the days that have the greatest (or least) total viewing hours, and speculate why those days attract the most (or fewest) viewers. Display the graphs on a bulletin board titled "Tracking TV Time."

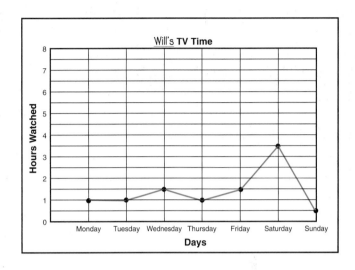

4. Extend It!

Invite students to explore double-line graphs with this group activity. Divide students into groups of eight to ten members, keeping the ratio of boys to girls as equal as possible. Give each group member a copy of page 67, a calculator, and access to a red and a blue colored pencil. Have each girl announce to her group how many hours she watched television on Monday. Each group member records this information on his copy of the girls' table. Direct the group to repeat this for the remaining days. Then, for each day, have every group member total the hours, divide by the number of girls, and write the resulting average (rounded to the nearest whole number) in the last column. Guide the group to complete the boys' table in a similar manner.

Next, instruct each group to complete the double-line graph to display the data (see the sample graph shown). Ask groups to discuss any differences between boys' and girls' viewing times and possible reasons for the differences. Invite groups to share their findings with the class.

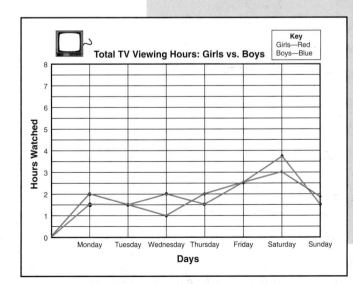

TV Watching Journal

_____'s Data

Day	Time(s) Watched		Total Hours
Monday	From _____ until _____	From _____ until _____	
Tuesday	From _____ until _____	From _____ until _____	
Wednesday	From _____ until _____	From _____ until _____	
Thursday	From _____ until _____	From _____ until _____	
Friday	From _____ until _____	From _____ until _____	
Saturday	From _____ until _____	From _____ until _____	
Sunday	From _____ until _____	From _____ until _____	
Week's Total: _____			

_____'s TV Time

Hours Watched

Monday Tuesday Wednesday Thursday Friday Saturday Sunday

Days

Note to the teacher: Use with pages 64 and 65.

Average Hours of TV Watched by Girls		
Day	Hours	Average
Monday		
Tuesday		
Wednesday		
Thursday		
Friday		
Saturday		
Sunday		

Average Hours of TV Watched by Boys		
Day	Hours	Average
Monday		
Tuesday		
Wednesday		
Thursday		
Friday		
Saturday		
Sunday		

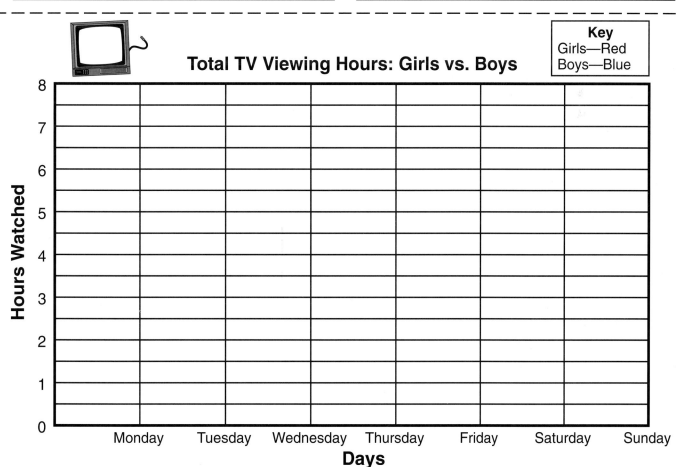

Total TV Viewing Hours: Girls vs. Boys

Key
Girls—Red
Boys—Blue

Hours Watched: 8, 7, 6, 5, 4, 3, 2, 1, 0

Days: Monday, Tuesday, Wednesday, Thursday, Friday, Saturday, Sunday

Note to the teacher: Use with "Extend It!" on page 65.

Spend, Spend, Spend!

Help students make "cents" of line graphs with a study of American spending habits!

Materials for Each Student
- copy of a data table from page 70
- two copies of page 71
- enlarged copy of the music sales table on page 69
- ruler
- colored pencils
- lined paper

1. Introduce It!

Enrich students' graphing skills by explaining that they will construct *line graphs* to show American spending habits. Review that a line graph shows how things change over time. Explain that after each student constructs her graph, she will draw conclusions about American spending habits.

2. Collect It! Display It!

To begin, provide each student with one of the data tables from page 70 and a copy of page 71. Have each student select one of the categories to graph. (Circulate around the room checking students' choices to make sure that all the categories have been selected at least once. Then instruct each student to study the greatest value for her data to help her number the vertical axis (see the example). Then guide the student to label her graph accordingly. Direct her to plot a point for the data for each year and then use a ruler to connect the points. Have her write a title that clearly tells what the graph is about. Remind her to include in parentheses how the data has been rounded.

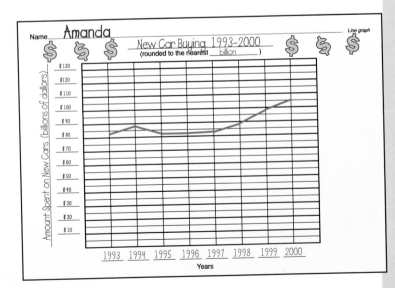

68   *Line graph*

3. Discuss It!

Next, ask each student to think about the changes in her data as shown on her completed graph. Prompt students' thinking with questions such as the following: How would you describe the slope of the line? If there is not much change in the slope, what does that tell you? *(The data did not change significantly over the years.)* If the slope climbs sharply, what does that tell you? *(The data increased over the years.)* What does it mean if the line goes up and down? *(The data increased and decreased over the years.)* Then ask leading questions to help students draw conclusions about their data such as the following: What is the difference between the number of CD singles sold in 1994 and the number sold in 1997? Why do you think more CD singles were sold in 1999 than in 1994? Guide students to share their conclusions with the class.

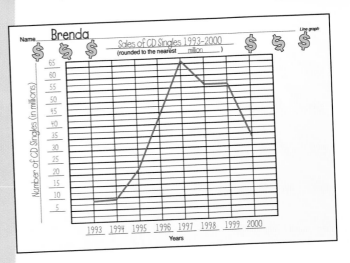

4. Extend It!

Give each student more practice with line graphs by having her construct a graph about the sales of her favorite type of music. Provide each student with an enlarged copy of the music sales table on this page, a copy of page 71, colored pencils, and a ruler. Explain that the table shows what percentage of all recorded music sales were made up by each genre, or category, of music. (For example, country music made up 17 percent of all music sales in 1995.)

Next, have each student choose a genre of music. Direct her to construct a line graph to show that genre's percentage of music sales for each year. When each graph is complete, ask the student to think about how the popularity of her genre has changed over time. Then ask her to predict how the sales percentages might have changed each year since 2000. Direct her to plot each year and prediction in colored pencil on her graph and then connect the points with the colored pencil. Encourage each student to share her graph and explain her predictions.

Percent of All Music Sales by Genre
(rounded to the nearest whole percent)

Category	1995	1996	1997	1998	1999	2000
Rock	34%	33%	33%	26%	25%	25%
Rap	7%	9%	10%	10%	11%	13%
Pop	10%	9%	9%	10%	10%	11%
Country	17%	15%	14%	14%	11%	11%
Rhythm and Blues	11%	12%	11%	13%	11%	10%
Classical	3%	3%	3%	3%	4%	3%

Number of Cell Phone Subscribers
(rounded to the nearest million)

1993............16 million
1994............24 million
1995............34 million
1996............44 million
1997............55 million
1998............69 million
1999............86 million
2000............109 million

Number of Compact Discs Sold
(rounded to the nearest ten million)

1993............500 million
1994............660 million
1995............720 million
1996............780 million
1997............750 million
1998............850 million
1999............940 million
2000............940 million

Number of Compact Disc Singles Sold
(rounded to the nearest million)

1993............8 million
1994............9 million
1995............22 million
1996............43 million
1997............67 million
1998............56 million
1999............56 million
2000............34 million

Number of Cassette Tapes Sold
(rounded to the nearest ten million)

1993............340 million
1994............350 million
1995............270 million
1996............230 million
1997............170 million
1998............160 million
1999............120 million
2000............80 million

Amount Spent on New Automobiles
(rounded to the nearest billion)

1993............$82 billion
1994............$87 billion
1995............$82 billion
1996............$82 billion
1997............$83 billion
1998............$88 billion
1999............$98 billion
2000............$105 billion

Amount Spent on Audio, Video, and Computer Goods
(rounded to the nearest billion)

1993............$63 billion
1994............$71 billion
1995............$77 billion
1996............$80 billion
1997............$84 billion
1998............$90 billion
1999............$98 billion
2000............$107 billion

Total Amount Spent on Food
(rounded to the nearest ten billion)

1993............$700 billion
1994............$730 billion
1995............$760 billion
1996............$790 billion
1997............$810 billion
1998............$850 billion
1999............$900 billion
2000............$960 billion

Amount Spent on Purchased Meals and Beverages
(rounded to the nearest ten billion)

1993............$260 billion
1994............$270 billion
1995............$290 billion
1996............$300 billion
1997............$320 billion
1998............$340 billion
1999............$350 billion
2000............$380 billion

Amount Spent on Clothes and Shoes
(rounded to the nearest ten billion)

1993............$230 billion
1994............$240 billion
1995............$250 billion
1996............$260 billion
1997............$270 billion
1998............$280 billion
1999............$300 billion
2000............$320 billion

Amount Spent on Recreation Services
(rounded to the nearest ten billion)

1993............$150 billion
1994............$160 billion
1995............$180 billion
1996............$190 billion
1997............$210 billion
1998............$220 billion
1999............$240 billion
2000............$260 billion

Note to the teacher: Use with pages 68 and 69.

Line graph

Name _____

$ $ $ $ $

_____
(rounded to the nearest _____)

Years

$ $

©The Education Center, Inc. • *Gotta Have Graphs!* • TEC60780

Note to the teacher: Use with pages 68 and 69.

Tracking Temperature Forecasts

Success is in the forecast with this multiple-line graph activity!

Materials
- copy of pages 74 and 75 for each student
- copy of the directions shown at the bottom of this page
- 7 consecutive days of newspaper weather reports
- ruler for each student
- large manila envelope
- colored pencils

1. Introduce It!
Breeze into this activity by asking students to think about the weather in your area. Then ask them to speculate what the weather is like in other parts of the world. Explain that they will construct *multiple-line graphs* to compare temperature forecasts from around the world. Inform students that a multiple-line graph compares how two or more sets of data change over time.

2. Collect It!
To prepare, collect newspaper weather reports that include local and world forecasts for seven consecutive days (or refer to a reliable weather Web site). Label the reports "Day 1" through "Day 7." Highlight the current day's local and world high temperature forecasts on each report. Staple the reports in order. Place the reports, colored pencils, a large envelope, student copies of page 74, and a copy of the directions below at a designated workspace. Have each student follow the directions below to collect the temperature data and fill in his table. Then tell the student to leave his completed table in the envelope for later use.

Directions to complete the table:
1. Record the first and last date of the weather reports in the spaces provided.
2. Write the name of the city in which you live.
3. Write the names of two selected foreign cities from the world temperature reports.
4. Referring to Day 1's local forecast, record that day's high temperature.
5. Referring to the world forecast, record the high temperature for each foreign city from Step 3.
6. Repeat Steps 4 and 5 for the remaining daily reports.

3. Display It! Discuss It!

After all the students have collected their data, guide them to graph the temperatures. To do this, direct each student visiting the center to retrieve his copy of page 74 from the envelope. Then have him write each city's name in the key, choose a different color for each city, and use the corresponding color to trace the dotted line next to the city's name. Next, have the student plot the first city's forecasted temperatures. Instruct each student to use a ruler and the appropriate color to connect the points. Then have him repeat this process for each of the remaining cities.

Next, lead each student to compare the temperatures from one city to the next. Ask the student to determine if any city had more temperature fluctuations. Also have the student look for any trends in the data. Allow each student to share his graph and his observations with a partner. Then invite students to suggest additional types of data they might display on multiple-line graphs.

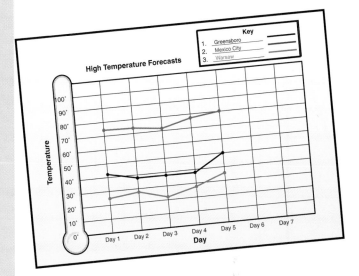

4. Extend It!

Give students more practice with multiple-line graphs by having them compare a five-day forecast with the actual temperatures. Collect the local weather report from your newspaper for six days (or refer to a reliable weather Web site to gather the forecasted and actual temperatures). Label the reports "Day 1" through "Day 6." Place the weather reports along with colored pencils, a ruler, and student copies of page 75 at a designated workspace. Direct each student to fill in the table on page 75 with the forecasted high temperatures for Day 1 through Day 5. Then, to find Day 1's actual temperature, have the student flip to the Day 2 report, locate the actual high temperature from the day before (sometimes labeled "Yesterday's Temperatures"), and record the temperature. Have the student repeat this process for Day 2 through Day 5.

Next, tell each student to complete the graph's title on page 75 by writing the city's name and weather report dates in the space provided. Instruct him to complete the key and then graph the forecasted and actual high temperatures. Ask the student to study his graph. Guide him to compare the line showing the forecast with the line showing the actual temperatures. Challenge students to evaluate the accuracy of the weekly forecast.

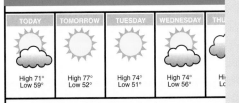

Name _____   *Multiple-line graph*

Temperatures Around the World

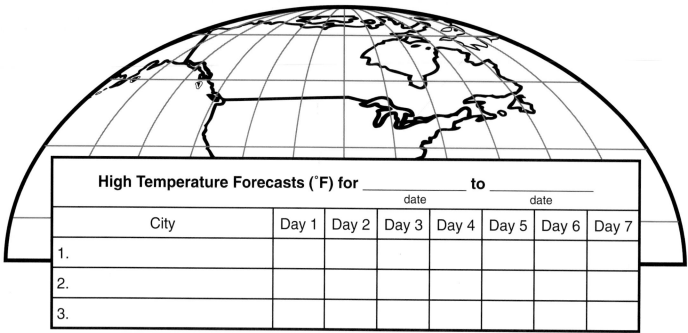

| High Temperature Forecasts (°F) for _____ to _____ | | | | | | | |
City	Day 1	Day 2	Day 3	Day 4	Day 5	Day 6	Day 7
1.							
2.							
3.							

Key

1. _____   _ _ _ _ _ _
2. _____   _ _ _ _ _ _
3. _____   _ _ _ _ _ _

High Temperature Forecasts

Temperature

100°
90°
80°
70°
60°
50°
40°
30°
20°
10°
0°

Day 1   Day 2   Day 3   Day 4   Day 5   Day 6   Day 7

Day

Note to the teacher: Use with pages 72 and 73.

Name _____

Following the Forecast

Forecast and Actual Temperatures (°F)

_____'s

for _____ to _____
      (city)

_____ date _____ date

	High Temperature Forecast	Actual High Temperature
Day 1		
Day 2		
Day 3		
Day 4		
Day 5		

Key

Forecast -------

Actual - - - - -

Temperature

100°
90°
80°
70°
60°
50°
40°
30°
20°
10°
0°

Day 1   Day 2   Day 3   Day 4   Day 5

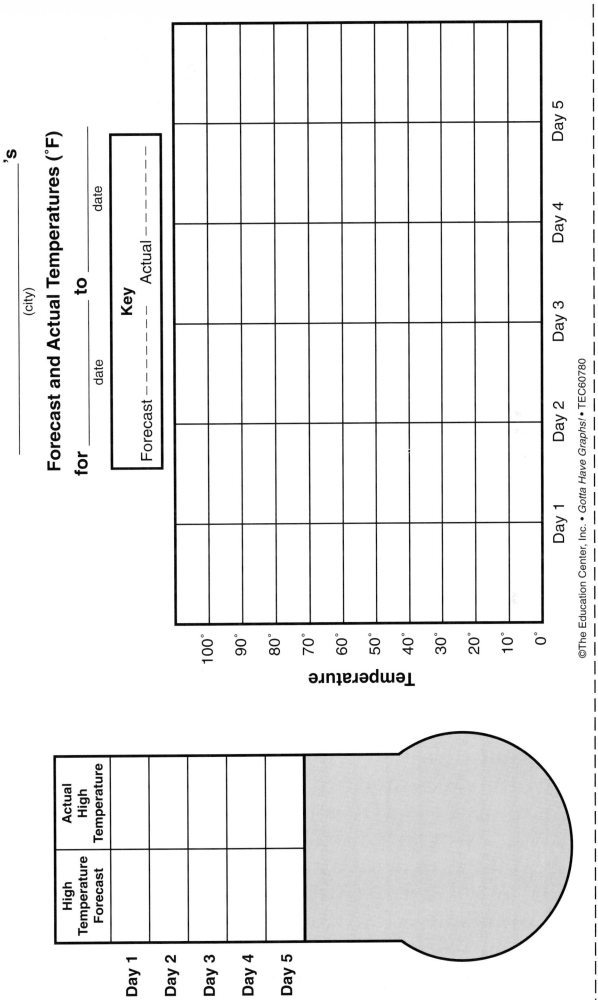

©The Education Center, Inc. • *Gotta Have Graphs!* • TEC60780

Note to the teacher: Use with "Extend It!" on page 73.

75

Scoring With Circle Graphs

When it comes to making circle graphs, this activity gives students a sporting chance!

Materials for Each Student

- copy of pages 78 and 79
- white, red, blue, yellow, green, and purple crayons
- scissors
- glue
- 9" x 12" sheet of construction paper

Hmmm.... Which is my favorite—football, soccer, baseball, basketball, golf, swimming, tennis, skiing, skating?

1. Introduce It!

Kick off the activity by reminding students that a *circle graph* (also called a pie graph) shows the relationship between a whole circle and the various slices into which it is divided. Then announce that each student will be constructing a circle graph that shows her classmates' favorite sports.

2. Collect It!

Give each child a copy of page 78 along with red, blue, yellow, green, and purple crayons. Have her cut apart the two parts of the reproducible, setting aside the circle graph patterns for later use. Then tell her to study the table and list in the first column four sports her classmates might name if asked, "What is your favorite sport?" Explain that the response "Other" is included in case a student's favorite sport is not among the ones listed. Then have the students rotate their papers along an established classroom path, directing each child to make a tally mark on the table to show her favorite sport. After ten rotations, have students return the papers back to their original owners.

3. Display It! Discuss It!

Next, point out the third column on the table. Ask students to explain why ten is the denominator for all of the fractions. *(Ten students were surveyed.)* Have each child write a fraction for each sport, using the total number of tally marks for the numerator.

To make a circle graph, give each student scissors, a white crayon, glue, and a 9" x 12" sheet of construction paper. Tell her to list the sports in the color code box on page 78 and then color each box a different color. Direct her to color a corresponding number of adjacent sections on the circle (page 78) to represent each fraction in the table. Finally, instruct each student to cut out the circle and color code box and glue them to the construction paper. Tell her to add a title, and then sign her name. When everyone is finished, have each child share her circle graph with the class, using the results to describe the surveyed students' favorite sports. Extend the discussion by asking whether the data might have differed if the students had surveyed a larger (or an older) group. Then display students' graphs on a bulletin board titled "Rounding Up Favorite Sports."

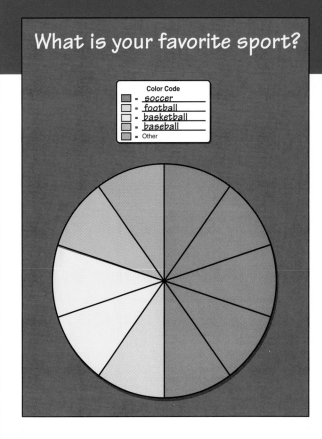

What is your favorite sport?

Color Code
- soccer
- football
- basketball
- baseball
- Other

Sample Survey Questions
What sport do you watch most on TV?
Who is your favorite living athlete?
What is your least favorite sport?
Which type of sport do you prefer: team or individual?

4. Extend It!

Students will have a ball brainstorming their own sports-related questions! Tell students that they are going to design surveys to learn about their classmates' sporting preferences. Give each child a copy of page 79. Guide students through Steps 1 and 2 on the page. (If desired, share the sample survey questions provided with students who need help brainstorming.) For Step 3, arrange for students to rotate their papers among 12 classmates, with each student making a tally mark for her response. When the papers are returned, have each student complete Steps 4 and 5 to construct a circle graph for the results. Arrange for each child to share her graph with a partner.

Circle Graph Patterns
Use with pages 76 and 77.

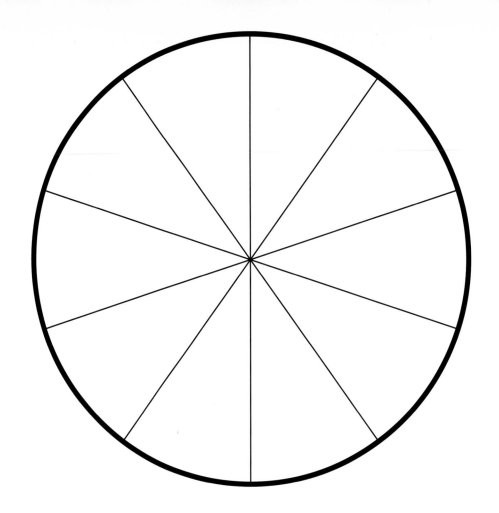

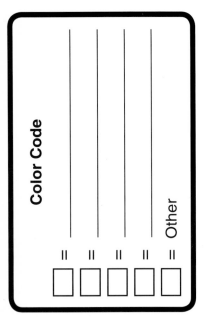

Color Code

|| _____

|| _____

|| _____

|| _____

= Other

Name _____   *Circle graph*

Winning Sports

Sport	Tally Marks	Fraction
		$\dfrac{}{10}$
		$\dfrac{}{10}$
		$\dfrac{}{10}$
		$\dfrac{}{10}$
Other		$\dfrac{}{10}$

Note to the teacher: Use with pages 76 and 77.

Name_____

Sporty Selections

Step 1 Write a sports-related question on the line below.

Survey question: _____

Step 2 In the table's first column, list up to four possible responses for the question you wrote in Step 1. Write the same responses on the lines in the color code box in Step 5.

Step 3 Pass your paper to 12 classmates. Have each student make a tally mark to show his or her response.

Step 4 For each fraction in the table, write a numerator that equals the total number of corresponding tally marks.

Answer	Tally Marks	Fraction
		$\frac{}{12}$
		$\frac{}{12}$
		$\frac{}{12}$
		$\frac{}{12}$
Other		$\frac{}{12}$

Step 5 Color each box in the color code a different color. Then color a corresponding number of sections in the circle to match each fraction. Title your circle graph.

Color Code

☐ = _____
☐ = _____
☐ = _____
☐ = _____
☐ = Other

title
_____

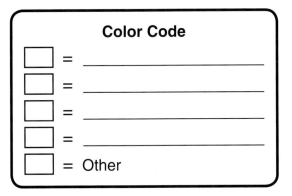

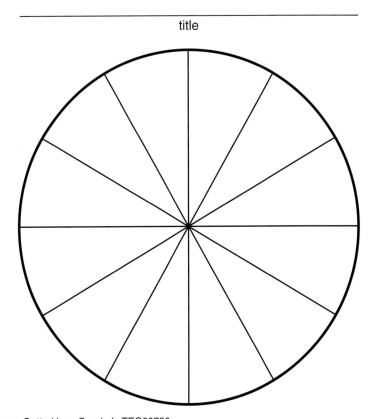

Circle Graphs by the Slice

Any way you slice it, this circle graph activity is sure to deliver!

Materials

- copy of pages 82 and 83 for each student
- extra copies of the pizza slice and key on page 82
- 8" paper circle for each student
- 12" x 18" sheet of construction paper for each group
- 12" x 18" sheet of construction paper for each student
- half sheet of lined paper for each student
- markers
- glue
- scissors

1. Introduce It!

Whet students' appetites for graphing by first asking them to imagine that they are ordering pizza for eight guests. Have them think about whether they should order pizza slices with cheese, vegetable, meat, or combined meat and vegetable toppings. Point out to students that they should first find out which toppings each person prefers. Inform them that they will construct *circle graphs* to show their guests' preferences. Explain that a circle graph shows the parts of a whole and the relationships among those parts.

2. Collect It!

To make sure you have enough topping preference data for the activity, ask several colleagues in advance about their pizza topping preferences. For each colleague, draw one symbol for each preferred topping on a copy of the pizza slice. Cut out the slices and set them aside. To begin the activity, divide students into groups of eight, forming partial groups as needed. Give each student a copy of page 82. Direct each child to draw one symbol for each of his preferred toppings on the pizza slice. Have him cut out the slice. (If necessary, use your colleagues' pizza slices to supplement any partial groups or to provide data for students who do not eat pizza.) Have each group assemble its pizza slices on a sheet of construction paper and then glue the resulting pizza in place.

Next, instruct each student to use the table on page 82 to mark each person's topping choices. When he is finished, have him code every person's preferences. Then tell him to record the appropriate fraction for each type of pizza in the space provided.

3. Display It! Discuss It!

To help students make circle graphs for their data, provide each child with an eight-inch paper circle. Tell him to fold it in half three times and then unfold it to reveal eight sections. Direct him to color the sections to show the fractional part of each type of pizza, using a different color for each type. Have group members compare their resulting graphs to ensure accuracy, making adjustments as needed. Then instruct each student to glue his circle graph to the top of a vertically positioned sheet of construction paper. Tell him to write a title for the graph and label the sections accordingly.

Next, on a half sheet of lined paper, instruct each child to write a paragraph that tells about his graph and explains how it can be used to order pizza for his group. Have him glue his writing below his graph. Then ask a representative from each group to share his graph with the class. Invite the remaining group members to share their writing. Display each student's work on a bulletin board titled "Circle Graphs by the Slice!"

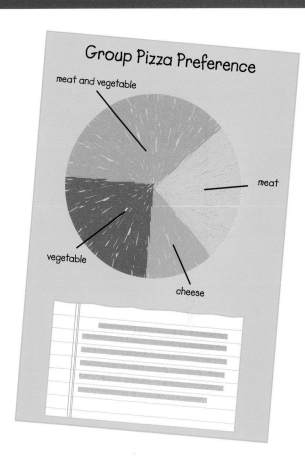

Group Pizza Preference

4. Extend It!

Top off students' exploration of circle graphs with this cool ice-cream survey! Provide each student with a copy of page 83. Guide him through the directions to survey his classmates and construct a circle graph. Arrange for each student to share his results with a partner.

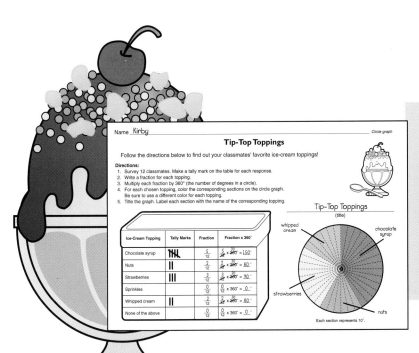

Name _____

Survey by the Slice

Name _____

Pizza Topping

Pizza Topping								
Pepperoni ◯								
Sausage ⌒								
Hamburger ꙮ								
Onion ◇								
Mushrooms ♤								
Peppers □								
Cheese ◖								
Pizza Type								

Pizza Type Code

M = Meat   V = Vegetable   MV = Meat and vegetable   C = Cheese

Type of Pizza	Fraction
Meat	
Vegetable	
Meat and vegetable	
Cheese	

Note to the teacher: Use with pages 80 and 81.

Pizza Slice Pattern
Use with pages 80 and 81.

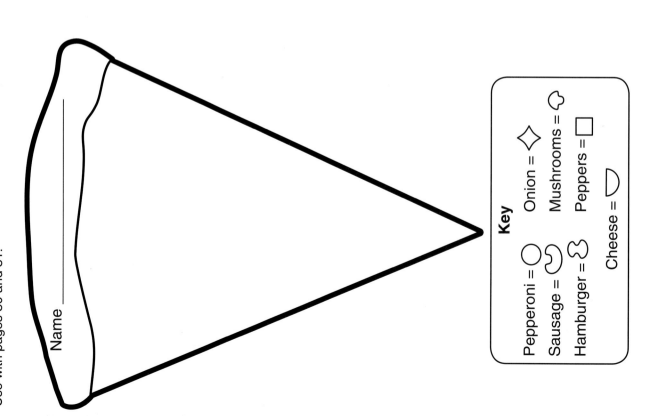

Name _____

Key

Pepperoni = ◯   Onion = ◇
Sausage = ⌒   Mushrooms = ♤
Hamburger = ꙮ   Peppers = □
Cheese = ◖

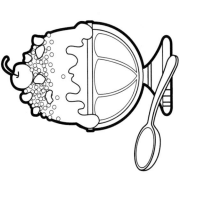

Tip-Top Toppings

Follow the directions below to find out your classmates' favorite ice-cream toppings!

Directions:
1. Survey 12 classmates. Make a tally mark on the table for each response.
2. Write a fraction for each topping.
3. Multiply each fraction by 360° (the number of degrees in a circle).
4. For each chosen topping, color the corresponding sections on the circle graph.
   Be sure to use a different color for each topping.
5. Title the graph. Label each section with the name of the corresponding topping.

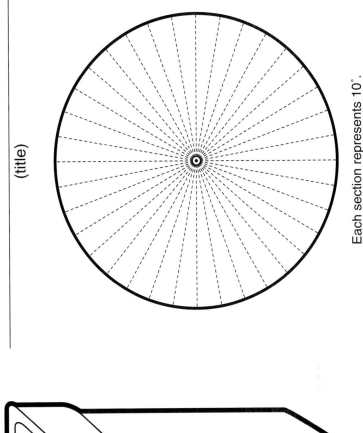

(title)

Each section represents 10°.

Ice-Cream Topping	Tally Marks	Fraction	Fraction x 360°
Chocolate syrup		$\overline{12}$	$\overline{12}$ x 360° = _____°
Nuts		$\overline{12}$	$\overline{12}$ x 360° = _____°
Strawberries		$\overline{12}$	$\overline{12}$ x 360° = _____°
Sprinkles		$\overline{12}$	$\overline{12}$ x 360° = _____°
Whipped cream		$\overline{12}$	$\overline{12}$ x 360° = _____°
None of the above		$\overline{12}$	$\overline{12}$ x 360° = _____°

©The Education Center, Inc. • *Gotta Have Graphs!* • TEC60780

Note to the teacher: Use with "Extend It!" on page 81.

Temperature Highs and Lows

What's in the forecast? A study of stem-and-leaf plots!

Materials
- copy of pages 86 and 87 for each student
- highlighter for each pair
- weather page from a newspaper for each pair

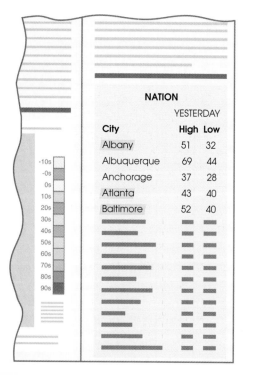

NATION		
	YESTERDAY	
City	High	Low
Albany	51	32
Albuquerque	69	44
Anchorage	37	28
Atlanta	43	40
Baltimore	52	40

-10s
-0s
0s
10s
20s
30s
40s
50s
60s
70s
80s
90s

1. Introduce It!

Warm students up to the activity by asking them to estimate yesterday's temperatures. Referring to the current day's weather page from a local newspaper, share the actual temperatures from the previous day. Then announce that each student is going to use data from the weather page of a newspaper to create a *stem-and-leaf plot* about the high and low temperatures for ten cities. Explain that a stem-and-leaf plot shows numerical data in such a way that the numbers themselves make up the display.

2. Collect It!

To begin, pair students. Give each pair a highlighter and a weather page that shows high and low temperatures. Also give each partner a copy of page 86. Instruct the pair to highlight ten U.S. or world cities listed on the weather page. Tell one partner to circle "high" on her reproducible and the other partner to circle "low" on his reproducible. Guide each child to complete Step 2 on the reproducible. Then, referring to the temperatures, have each partner study the corresponding high or low values.

3. Display It! Discuss It!

Once the partners complete Steps 1 and 2, guide each child through Steps 3, 4, and 5 on page 86 to complete the stem-and-leaf plot. Demonstrate on the board how to use a number's tens digit to write a stem and its ones digit to write a leaf. Point out that stems and leaves are written in order from least to greatest, with the stems in a column to the left of the dividing line and the leaves in rows to the right. *(Inform students that if duplicate tens digits occur, they should only list it once on the plot.)* Instruct the student to write a title and complete the key to show the value of a selected stem and leaf. (See the example.)

When everyone is finished, have each pair study its plots to determine the lowest temperature and highest temperature. Then have students observe their plots to determine whether the low and high temperatures tended to cluster on the plots or whether they spread out more evenly on the plots. Call on pairs to share their findings. Then have students give reasons why some pairs may have found clusters of temperatures while others had more evenly dispersed temperatures. *(Pairs that selected cities in similar climates may find clusters of temperatures while pairs that selected cities from more diverse climates may find values spread out all over their plots.)* Conclude by having pairs share other interesting observations of their plots.

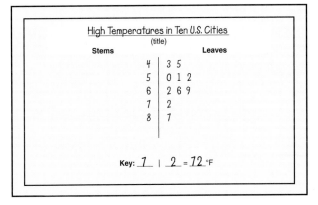

4. Extend It!

Who's watching the weather? Your students will be with this bar graph activity! On a weather page, point out the weather (or sky condition) abbreviations next to the city's temperatures. Also direct students' attention to the key that tells what each abbreviation means. Then give each pair a copy of page 87. Referring to the predicted conditions, instruct the pair to color a box on the graph for each of the ten cities the pair highlighted on its weather page that is expected to have that weather condition. Also have the pair write a title for the graph. Invite pairs to share their graphs with the class.

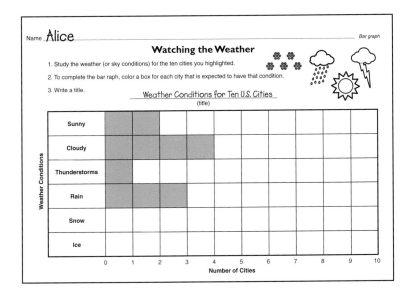

Keeping Tabs on the Temperature

Study the high or low temperature for the cities you highlighted on the weather page. Follow the steps below to create a stem-and-leaf plot.

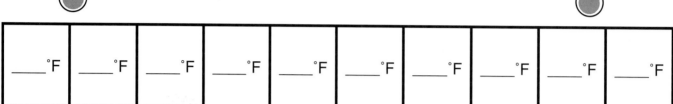

Step 1: Circle one.   High   Low

Step 2: If you circled "high" in Step 1, write the high temperatures for ten different cities. If you circled "low" write the low temperatures for ten different cities.

____°F	____°F	____°F	____°F	____°F	____°F	____°F	____°F	____°F	____°F

Step 3: List the temperatures in order.

Least   Greatest

____°F, ____°F, ____°F, ____°F, ____°F, ____°F, ____°F, ____°F, ____°F, ____°F

Step 4: List the stems (tens digits) in order from top to bottom. List the leaves (ones digits) for each stem from left to right.

_____
(title)

Stems   **Leaves**

Key: ____ | ____ = ____°F

Step 5: Write a title and complete the key.

Note to the teacher: Use with pages 84 and 85.

Name _____

Bar graph

Watching the **Weather**

1. Study the weather (or sky conditions) for the ten cities you highlighted.

2. To complete the bar graph, color a box for each city that is expected to have that condition.

3. Write a title.

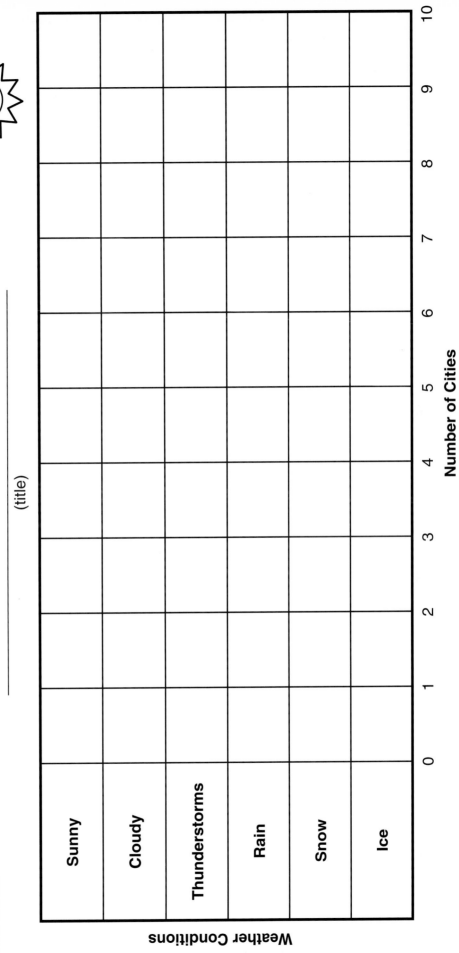

_____
(title)

Weather Conditions	0	1	2	3	4	5	6	7	8	9	10
Sunny											
Cloudy											
Thunderstorms											
Rain											
Snow											
Ice											

Number of Cities

©The Education Center, Inc. • *Gotta Have Graphs!* • TEC60780

Note to the teacher: Use with "Extend It!" on page 85.

Major-League Displays

Students step up to the plate and construct stem-and-leaf plots with this grand-slam activity!

Materials for Each Student
- copy of pages 90 and 91 for each student
- copy of major league home run statistics

1. Introduce It!

Invite students to take a swing at naming major-league players who have set home run records. Then tell students that they are going to construct *stem-and-leaf plots* to display home run record data. Explain that unlike most data displays, a stem-and-leaf plot actually uses the numerical data collected to create the display.

2. Collect It! Display It!

To lead students in collecting the data, give each child a copy of page 90. Also provide him with a copy of major-league home run records from an almanac or another resource. Instruct him to select ten consecutive years of records. In the table at the top of page 90, have him fill in the league name, the time span, and the home run records. Then have him list the numbers in order from least to greatest value. Next, guide him through the directions below to complete the stem-and-leaf plot at the bottom of page 90.

Directions:
1. Write a title for the plot.
2. On the plot, separate each value (home run record) into stems and leaves. To do this, list the tens digits of the home run records in the stems column from least to greatest (top to bottom). (If duplicate tens digits occur, only list them once on the plot.) Then list the ones digits from each home run record in the leaves column from least to greatest (left to right).
3. Complete the key by choosing any value from the plot. Write the value as a stem and a leaf; then write the number it represents.

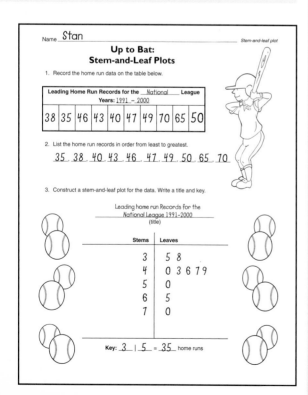

Name _Stan_

Stem-and-leaf plot

Up to Bat:
Stem-and-Leaf Plots

1. Record the home run data on the table below.

Leading Home Run Records for the _National_ League Years: _1991 – 2000_									
38	35	46	43	40	47	49	70	65	50

2. List the home run records in order from least to greatest.

_35_ , _38_ , _40_ , _43_ , _46_ , _47_ , _49_ , _50_ , _65_ , _70_

3. Construct a stem-and-leaf plot for the data. Write a title and key.

Leading home run Records for the
National League 1991-2000
(title)

Stems	Leaves
3	5 8
4	0 3 6 7 9
5	0
6	5
7	0

Key: _3_ | _5_ = _35_ home runs

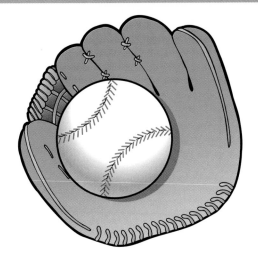

3. Discuss It!

After students have completed their plots, have them study the plots to determine the lowest number of home runs for the span of years researched. Then have students observe their plots to determine whether the home run records tended to cluster or whether they spread out evenly on the plot. Call on students to share their findings. Also have students share other interesting observations of their plots.

4. Extend It!

Which league has the best home run hitters—the National League or the American League? Challenge students to find out by constructing *back-to-back stem-and-leaf plots*. To begin, divide students so that there are ten groups (or pairs). Give each student a copy of page 91 and access to the home run records. Assign each group a ten-year span (beginning with 1901–1910) and have each group member record the years on his copy of the table. Then guide students through the provided directions to complete their plots.

When the displays are finished, have the students in each group analyze their plots and share their findings with the class. After all the data has been shared, invite students to discuss which league has higher home run records. Batter up!

Directions:
1. Record the home run data on the table provided on page 91.
2. List the home run records for each league from least to greatest.
3. Study the records for both leagues. Circle the least and greatest values.
4. In the stems column, list the tens digits from least to greatest (top to bottom). (If duplicate tens digits occur, list them only once.)
5. Study the records for the National League. In the leaves column on the left, list the ones digits for each stem from least to greatest (right to left).
6. Study the records for the American League. In the leaves column on the right, list the ones digits for each stem from least to greatest (left to right).
7. Write a title.
8. To complete the key, choose any stem value and a corresponding leaf value from each league. Write the values in the spaces provided; then write the value of the two numbers.

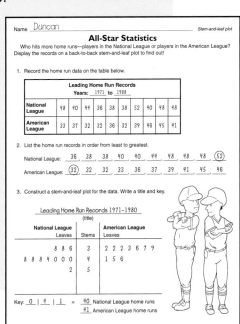

Up to Bat:
Stem-and-Leaf Plots

1. Record the home run data on the table below.

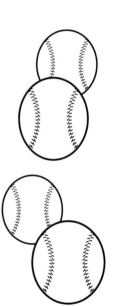

Leading Home Run Records for the _____ League Years: _____ – _____									

2. List the home run records in order from least to greatest.

_____, _____, _____, _____, _____, _____, _____, _____, _____, _____

3. Construct a stem-and-leaf plot for the data. Write a title and key.

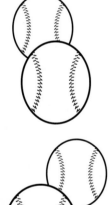

_____
(title)

Stems	Leaves

Key: _____ | _____ = _____ home runs

Name _____

All-Star Statistics

Who hits more home runs—players in the National League or players in the American League? Display the records on a back-to-back stem-and-leaf plot to find out!

1. Record the home run data on the table below.

Leading Home Run Records Years: _____ to _____									
National League									
American League									

2. List the home run records in order from least to greatest.

   National League: _____, _____, _____, _____, _____, _____, _____, _____, _____, _____

   American League: _____, _____, _____, _____, _____, _____, _____, _____, _____, _____

3. Construct a stem-and-leaf plot for the data. Write a title and key.

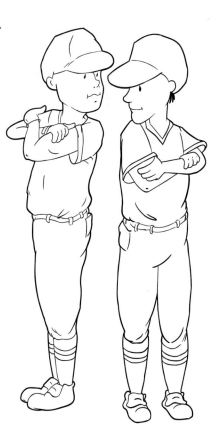

_____
(title)

National League Leaves	Stems	**American League** Leaves

Key: ___ | ___ | ___ = _____ National League home runs
                              _____ American League home runs

Histograms by the Book

This investigation of chapter book pages is sure to result in a happy ending!

Materials for Each Student

- copy of pages 94 and 95
- ruler
- 4 index cards
- black marker
- crayons
- tape
- pencil

1. Introduce It!

To open this page-turning activity, prompt students to think about the chapter books they have read. Ask them to predict the average number of pages in a chapter book. Have each child write her prediction on a provided copy of page 94. Then inform students that a *histogram* is a type of bar graph that shows the number of times data occurs within intervals, or a range of numbers. Tell students that they will construct histograms to show the number of pages in chapter books.

2. Collect It!

To provide access to a variety of books, arrange for students to visit the school library. Have each child bring a copy of page 94, a ruler, and a pencil. At the library, instruct each student to select a chapter book and use the ruler to hold its place on the shelf. Instruct her to record the book title and number of pages in the space provided on page 94. Tell her to replace the book and retrieve her ruler. Direct her to repeat this process with three additional books.

3. Display It! Discuss It!

Upon returning to the classroom, divide students into small groups. Have the members within each group study their page totals. Instruct each group to cross out page totals for any repeated book titles. Then, using the directions on page 94, guide the group to determine the appropriate intervals for the page totals. Explain that the quotient found in the first step should be used as a guideline for determining the range. (For example, if the largest page total is 309, divide 309 by 5, the number of intervals. The quotient is 61 R4. The range might be 69 with the following intervals: 0–69, 70–139, etc.)

Next, give each student a copy of page 95. Have each group work together to choose a reasonable scale for the histogram. Tell each student to number the axes accordingly, write a title, and graph the data. (Remind students that the bars should touch.) Then instruct each child to answer the questions that follow. Have the members within each group share their answers.

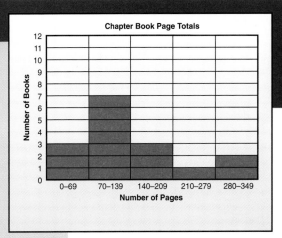

4. Extend It!

Combine the group data to show students how page totals really stack up! Point out that each group's data represents only a small sample of all the books in the library. Further explain that the larger the sample, the more likely the results will represent the actual page totals. Then inform students that they will combine their page totals to make a class histogram. To do this, have students help determine the greatest page total in the class. Divide this number by the number of desired intervals to determine the range for each interval. Use a black marker to list each interval on a separate index card. Display the cards at the bottom of a wall space in a horizontal row as shown.

Next, give each student four index cards. Have her use a black marker to write each book title and page total on a different card. Individually invite students to tape each card in the appropriate column on the histogram, discarding any cards for duplicate book titles. After all the cards have been posted, title and label the resulting histogram. Ask students to compare the display with their group histograms. Invite them to share their observations.

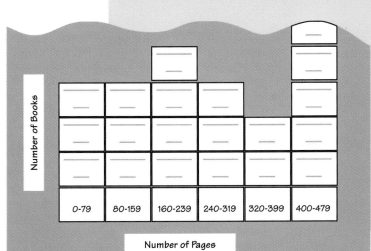

Reading Into Data

Predict: On average, how many pages do you think are in a chapter book?

Select a chapter book. Record the title and page number in the space provided. Repeat this with a total of four books. Then follow the directions to complete the frequency table.

My prediction is

_____ pages.

Title 1:

_____

Page total: _____

Title 2:

_____

Page total: _____

Title 3:

_____

Page total: _____

Title 4:

_____

Page total: _____

Directions:

1. Divide the greatest page total from your group's data by 5. ____ ÷ 5 = _____
2. Use the quotient to help determine the range for each interval. Write the intervals in the table, starting the first interval with 0.
3. Make a tally mark for each page total in your group, without repeating book titles.
4. Write the frequency (total) for each interval.

Interval					
Tally Marks					
Frequency					

A Page-Turning Histogram

Study the results from the frequency table on page 94. Display the data on the histogram.

_____
(title)

Number of Books

0

_____   _____   _____   _____   _____

Number of Pages

Questions:

1. How many books are represented on the histogram? _____

2. Within which interval are the most books? _____   The least books? _____

3. How does the data compare to your prediction? _____

_____

4. If you randomly selected a book from the library, about how many pages would you expect it to have? _____   Explain. _____

_____

5. How might the histogram look different if it showed the page totals for picture books?

_____

_____

Note to the teacher: Use with pages 92 and 93.

Auto Ads

Steer students toward a clear understanding of histograms with this fun activity!

Materials for Each Student

- copy of page 98
- two copies of page 99
- colored pencils
- access to used-car section from classified ads

1. Introduce It!

Get students revved up for *histograms* by asking them to estimate how much a used car costs. Point out that on average, certain makes of cars are usually more expensive than others. Then explain to students that they will construct histograms to show the prices of the used cars advertised in the local newspaper. Remind students that this type of bar graph shows the number of times data occurs within intervals or ranges of numbers.

2. Collect It!

In advance, gather the classified ads from several newspapers. Divide students into small groups. Give each group the ads and student copies of the Car Price Tally Table on page 98. Assign each group a different car make (such as Honda or Ford). Instruct each group member to write the car make at the top of the table. Then have the group appoint one member to locate ads for those cars in the classified ads. (Confirm that students locate regular automobiles and not trucks or utility vehicles.) Tell the appointed student to read aloud each price to his group. As he does so, have each member make a tally mark on the table for each price in the corresponding space. (Instruct the readers to make tally marks on their tables too.)

Name Ralph   *Histogram*

Used Car Prices

Car Make BMW

Car Prices	Tally Marks	Car Prices	Tally Marks
$0–$9,999	卌 I	$50,000–$59,999	II
$10,000–$19,999	III	$60,000–$69,999	I
$20,000–$29,999	卌 III	$70,000–$79,999	
$30,000–$39,999	I	$80,000–$89,999	
$40,000–$49,999		$90,000–$99,999	

3. Display It! Discuss It!

To display the data, give each student a copy of page 99 and have him title the graph. Tell him to study the data he collected on the table and then number the vertical axis accordingly. Have him write a heading for both axes in the space provided. Instruct him to color the histogram to show his data. Encourage the students within each group to compare histograms to ensure accuracy. Then have a representative from each group share the display with the class. Challenge students to compare the car prices for different makes. Building on their prior knowledge about the cars, invite them to share their conclusions. Use the provided questions to further students' interpretations of their histograms.

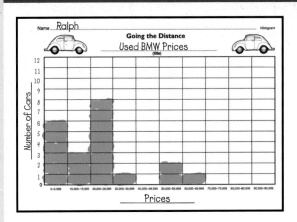

Questions

Study your histogram. Between which range of prices did most of the cars fall?

Which prices, if any, were extremely high or low?

Was there a significant difference in the car prices? Explain.

Who might be interested in the data you collected? *(Possible answer: someone selling or buying a used car)*

4. Extend It!

Now that students have a solid understanding of histograms, let them go the distance by studying car mileage! Give each student a copy of the mileage tally table on page 98. Have him take it home and ask permission to record the mileage that is on his family's car or on the car of someone he knows. (For the purposes of this study, ask students to collect mileages less than 100,000 miles.) Upon returning to the class, have each child announce the mileage he recorded. Tell

each student (including the one who announced the mileage) to make a tally mark for the data on the table in the corresponding space. Then give each child a copy of 99. Have him title and label the graph. Instruct him to color the bars to show the data. Discuss the results as a class.

Car Price Tally Table

Use with pages 96 and 97.

Name _____ *Histogram*

Used Car Prices

Car Make _____

Car Prices	Tally Marks	Car Prices	Tally Marks
$0–$9,999		$50,000–$59,999	
$10,000–$19,999		$60,000–$69,999	
$20,000–$29,999		$70,000–$79,999	
$30,000–$39,999		$80,000–$89,999	
$40,000–$49,999		$90,000–$99,999	

Mileage Tally Table

Use with "Extend It!" on page 97.

Name _____ *Histogram*

Miles to Go

Mileage: _____ miles

Mileage	Tally Marks	Mileage	Tally Marks
0–9,999		50,000–59,999	
10,000–19,999		60,000–69,999	
20,000–29,999		70,000–79,999	
30,000–39,999		80,000–89,999	
40,000–49,999		90,000–99,999	

Name

Going the Distance

(title)

| 0-9,999 | 10,000-19,999 | 20,000-29,999 | 30,000-39,999 | 40,000-49,999 | 50,000-59,999 | 60,000-69,999 | 70,000-79,999 | 80,000-89,999 | 90,000-99,999 |

0

Note to the teacher: Use with pages 96 and 97.

Letter-Perfect Plots

This great graphing activity can help students understand box-and-whisker plots all the way from A to Z!

Materials for Each Student

- copy of pages 102 and 103
- list of classmates' first and last names
- list of teachers' last names

Wow! My name has 14 letters!

Class List

	8
Greg Bell	8
Ben Smith	9
Dan Sharpe	10
Tasha Evans	9
Sue Walker	12
Sharon Murphy	13
Clevell Harris	9
Donna Teal	9
Harry Tate	

1. Introduce It!

To teach students the ABCs of constructing *box-and-whisker plots,* begin by telling them that this type of plot shows how data is distributed, or spread out. Then announce that each student will use the letters in her classmates' names to construct a box-and-whisker plot.

2. Collect It!

Explain to students that the first step in constructing a box-and-whisker plot is collecting the needed data. Give each child a list of her classmates' first and last names. (If you have an even number of students, add your name to the list to make the activity easier to do.) Instruct each student to count the number of letters in each person's first and last name and record the total next to the corresponding name.

3. Display It! Discuss It!

Once the letter totals have been recorded, give each child a copy of page 102. Read over and discuss the important terms listed on the page. Then use the following information to help them understand the components of the sample box-and-whisker plot.

- *Whiskers* (horizontal line segments) extending from the box's left and right sides represent the lower and upper 25 percent of the data, respectively.
- The endpoint on the box's left whisker represents the data's *lower extreme*.
- The endpoint on the box's right whisker represents the data's *upper extreme*.
- The point on the vertical line inside the box represents the data's *median*.
- The point on the vertical line forming the box's left side represents the data's *lower quartile*.
- The point on the vertical line forming the box's right side represents the data's *upper quartile*.

Next, guide each student to construct a box-and-whisker plot by completing page 102 as directed. When everyone is finished, have volunteers identify the plot's median, its lower and upper extremes, and its lower and upper quartiles. Then help students interpret the plot by having them answer questions such as the following: What is the average number of letters in the names? What is the highest total of letters? The lowest total? What is the average number of letters between the median and the upper extreme? Between the median and the lower extreme?

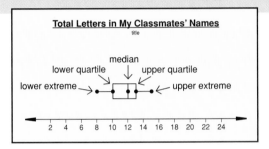

4. Extend It!

To explore another graph that shows how data is distributed, invite your students to construct line plots. Explain that a *line plot* shows numerical data plotted as Xs above a number line, making it easy to identify range and mode. To begin, provide each student with a list of teachers' last names. Have the student count the number of letters in each teacher's last name and record the total next to the corresponding name. Then give each child a copy of page 103. Guide her to construct a line plot by completing the page as directed. When students are finished, discuss the page's questions and answers together. Conclude by using the questions below to help students see how line plots and box-and-whisker plots are alike and different.

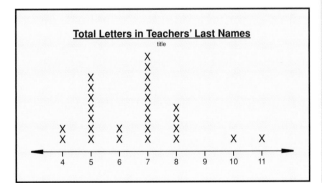

Questions
How are line plots and box-and-whisker plots alike? *(They both show the distribution of data, making it easy to identify the data's range.)*
How does a line plot differ from a box-and-whisker plot? *(A line plot's data is written vertically as Xs above a number line. The data for a box-and-whiskers plot is also shown above a number line, but its data is represented as a horizontal box with whiskers extending from its left and right sides.)*
Which plot makes it easier to identify mode? *(line plot)*
Which plot makes it easier to identify median? *(box-and-whisker plot)*

Letter-Perfect Plot

Carefully follow the steps below to construct a box-and-whisker plot similar to the one shown. As you complete each step, shade in the box next to it.

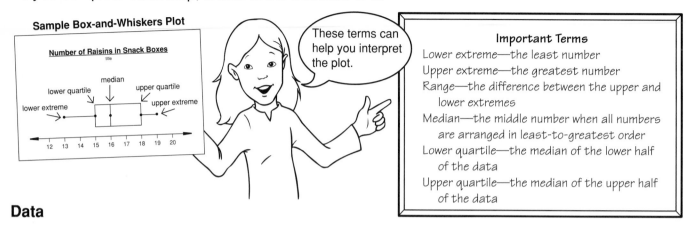

Important Terms

Lower extreme—the least number
Upper extreme—the greatest number
Range—the difference between the upper and lower extremes
Median—the middle number when all numbers are arranged in least-to-greatest order
Lower quartile—the median of the lower half of the data
Upper quartile—the median of the upper half of the data

Data

_____

_____

☐ 1. On the lines above, order the data you collected from least to greatest.

☐ 2. Circle the two numbers in your data that represent the lower and upper extremes. On the number line below, mark a black dot above each of the corresponding numbers. (If the lower and upper extremes are not on the number line, add them.)

☐ 3. Draw a triangle around the number from the data that represents the median. Mark a dot and draw a short vertical line above the corresponding number on the number line below. (If the median is not one of the numbers on the number line, add it.)

☐ 4. Draw an X on the number from your data that represents the lower quartile. Mark a dot and draw a short vertical line above the corresponding number on the number line below. (If the lower quartile is not one of the numbers on the line, add it.) Repeat to identify and label the upper quartile.

☐ 5. To construct the box, draw a pair of parallel lines to connect the vertical lines of the lower and upper quartiles.

☐ 6. To make the box's left whisker, draw a line that connects the box's left side to the black dot representing the lower extreme. Make the box's right whisker by drawing a line that connects the box's right side to the black dot representing the upper extreme.

☐ 7. Write a title for the plot on the line provided.

My Box-and-Whisker Plot

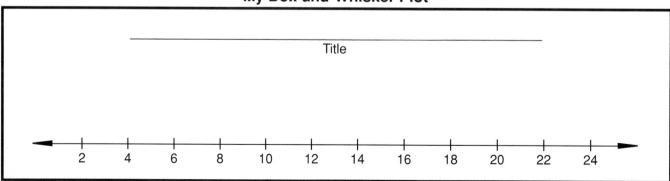

X Marks the Spot!

Follow the steps below to construct a line plot similar to the one shown. As you complete each step, shade the box next to it.

Sample Line Plot

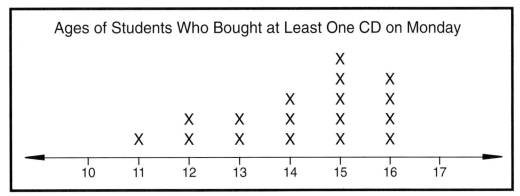

Ages of Students Who Bought at Least One CD on Monday

☐ 1. Label the marks on the line below with numbers to represent the range of your data.

☐ 2. Plot the data by placing an X on the line plot for each number in your data.

☐ 3. Write a title for the plot on the line provided.

My Line Plot

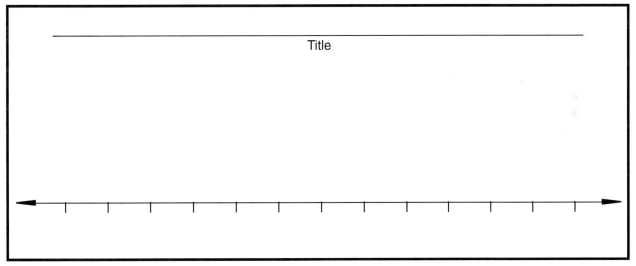

Title

Now use the line plot to answer these questions.

4. What is the median of this set of data? _____

5. What is the range of this set of data? _____

6. Is there a mode for this set of data? _____ Why or why not? _____

_____

_____

Sharp Plotting

Have students explore pencil lengths to investigate the finer points of box-and-whisker plots!

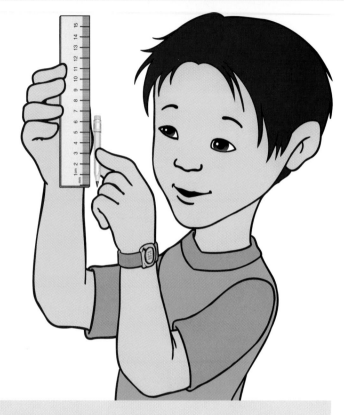

Materials for Each Student

- copy of pages 106 and 107
- supply of pencils
- supply of Unifix cubes
- ruler

Note: If students are unfamiliar with making box-and-whisker plots, have them complete the activities on pages 100–103 before completing this unit.

1. Introduce It!

Begin this activity on the "write" foot by having each student randomly select a pencil from his desk and estimate its length in centimeters. Invite students to speculate the average length of their classmates' pencils. Then explain that each student will construct a *box-and-whisker plot* to display the lengths. Remind students that a box-and-whisker plot shows how far apart and how evenly data is distributed, or spread out.

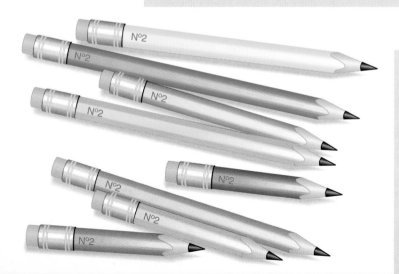

2. Collect It!

Next, give each student a ruler and a copy of page 106. Instruct him to gather all the pencils (not mechanical) from his desk. Tell him to measure each pencil to the nearest centimeter and record his findings in the space provided on page 106. Then divide students into small groups. Have each student write his group's compiled pencil lengths from shortest to longest in the space provided.

3. Display It! Discuss It!

Once the pencil lengths have been recorded, direct students' attention to the sample box-and-whisker plot on page 106. Confirm that students understand the plot's components as explained below. Then guide each student to construct a box-and-whisker plot to show the pencil lengths. When everyone is finished, have volunteers identify the plot's median, its lower and upper extremes, and its lower and upper quartiles. Then help students interpret the plot by having them answer questions such as the following: What is the average pencil length? What is the average pencil length between the median and the upper extreme? Between the median and the lower extreme?

Components of a Box-and-Whisker Plot

- *Whiskers* (horizontal line segments) extending from the box's left and right sides represent the lower and upper 25 percent of the data, respectively.
- The endpoint on the box's left whisker represents the data's *lower extreme.*
- The endpoint on the box's right whisker represents the data's *upper extreme.*
- The point on the vertical line inside the box represents the data's *median.*
- The point on the vertical line forming the box's left side represents the data's *lower quartile.*
- The point on the vertical line forming the box's right side represents the data's *upper quartile.*

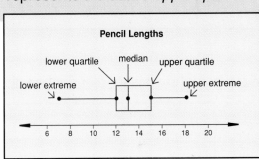

Pencil Lengths

4. Extend It!

This pencil inventory is sure to sharpen students' understanding of statistics! Give each child a copy of page 107. Ask him to predict how many pencils each student has in and on top of his desk. Tell him to write his prediction at the top of the page. Instruct him to gather all the pencils from his desk and count them. Have him write his name and total number of pencils on the table in Part 1 of his page. Then divide students into groups so that there is an odd number of students in each group. (If necessary, give your own pencil total to an even-numbered group to result in an odd number of values.) Have each student complete the table with his group members' pencil totals.

Next, give each group a supply of Unifix cubes. Have each group member select a different color. Tell him to take one cube for each pencil he has and then stack the cubes. Direct group members to study all the stacks. Guide them through the directions in Part 2 of the page to analyze the data. Then have students answer the questions that follow in Part 3. Discuss the answers as a class.

Pencil Plots

Measure each of your pencils to the nearest centimeter.
Write each length on the line below.

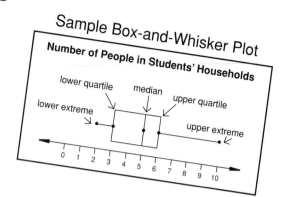

Sample Box-and-Whisker Plot
Number of People in Students' Households
lower quartile   median   upper quartile
lower extreme   upper extreme
0 1 2 3 4 5 6 7 8 9 10

My Pencil Lengths

_____

Now list all the pencil lengths from your group (including
your own) from shortest to longest.

Group Pencil Lengths

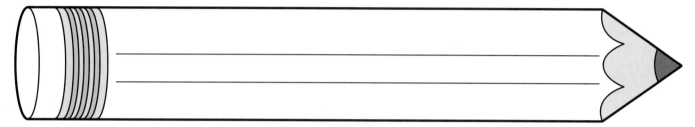

Make a box-and-whisker plot to show the pencil lengths.

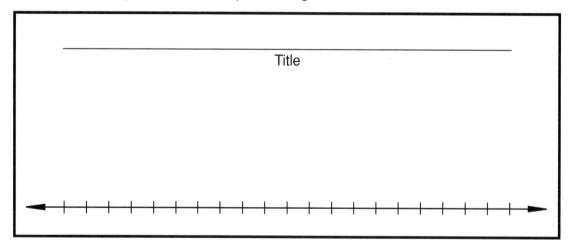

Title

Use your box-and-whisker plot to complete the following items.

1. What is the median length for the pencils in your group? _____

2. How long is the longest pencil? _____ The shortest pencil? _____

3. What is the range of the pencil lengths? _____

4. Identify a pencil length that falls within the lower quartile of the data. _____

5. Identify a pencil length that falls within the upper quartile of the data. _____

Sharp Statistics

Predict: How many pencils do you think each student has? _____

Part 1: Complete the table to show how many pencils each group member has.

Group Members	Number of Pencils

Part 2: Study the stacks of cubes in your group. Complete the items below to find each statistic.

1. Count the cubes in the tallest and shortest stacks. Subtract.
   Range: _____ − _____ = _____

2. Arrange the stacks from shortest to tallest. Count the cubes in the middle stack.
   Median: _____

3. List the number of cubes in any size of stack that appears most often.
   Mode(s): _____

4. Without changing the number of stacks, move cubes from one stack to another until each stack has about the same number of cubes. Count the cubes in each stack. Write the most frequent number.
   Mean: _____

Part 3: Answer the questions.

1. Compare your prediction to the mean, median, and mode. Which statistic (or statistics) is closest to your prediction, if any? Explain.

2. Describe how the statistics might be different if your group members counted their crayons or markers.

3. Imagine that another group member had a lot more pencils than anyone else in the group. On the back of this sheet, explain what effect this would have on each statistic, if any.

Note to the teacher: Use with "Extend It!" on page

Frosty Glyphs

Students are sure to warm up to displaying data on these cool snowman glyphs!

Materials

- copy of page 110 for each student
- copy of page 111 for each group
- class supply of 9" x 12" sheets of yellow and orange construction paper
- black, red, blue, and green crayons for each student
- scissors
- glue

1. Introduce It!

Warm up to this cold-weather investigation by explaining to your students that a *glyph* is a picture in which each part of the picture represents a different piece of information. Then explain that they are about to construct glyphs about their classmates' winter likes and dislikes.

2. Collect It!

Inform students that before constructing a glyph, information has to be collected. Give each student a copy of the survey on page 110. Tell your students that one way to collect information is by conducting a survey. Explain that a survey usually consists of asking a person a series of questions about a particular topic. Read over the survey with your students; then divide the students into pairs. Instruct one student in each pair to read the survey question to her partner and then circle the corresponding answer. Have the other partner repeat the process.

3. Display It! Discuss It!

After each pair has completed its surveys, provide each student with glue, scissors, crayons, and a copy of the snowman and broom patterns on page 110. Also make sure that the students have access to yellow and orange construction paper. Instruct each student to assemble a snowman glyph according to her partner's survey responses. Have the student use a black crayon to print her partner's name at the bottom of the paper so that it can be seen from a distance. Collect the snowman glyphs and display them in a prominent place in the classroom. Then have students look carefully at the glyphs. Invite volunteers to make statements about their classmate's cold-weather preferences using the survey questions to help them. Challenge students to find pairs of classmates whose glyphs contain the same preferences. Extend the discussion by asking, "Does where we live affect how our glyphs look? How might the glyphs be different for students living in another part of the country?"

4. Extend It!

For more advanced students, try the following bar graph activity. Divide students into four groups and provide each group with a copy of the bar graph on page 111. Number the groups 1 to 4, and then direct a designated recorder to write the corresponding survey question at the top of the graph. Have her write the question's responses on the lines at the bottom of the graph *(only survey question 4 will use each blank at the bottom of the graph)*. Instruct the group to count the data for each response on the snowman glyphs. For example, if the response to survey question 4 is ice-skating, have the group count the number of glyphs containing triangle buttons. Direct the recorder to color the bar graph accordingly. Post each group's graph near the posted glyphs. Then read each question below and have the class decide whether it is more appropriate to use the glyphs or graphs to answer the question. Lead students to understand that each glyph provides information about an individual while each graph shows information about a group of people.

Questions
How many students wear mittens? *(bar graph)*
Which activity does [student's name] like the best? *(glyph)*
How many students like hot chocolate and wear hats? *(glyph)*
How many students have never played in the snow? *(bar graph)*
Which students in our class like ice-skating the best? *(glyph)*

Snowman and Broom Patterns
Use with page 109.

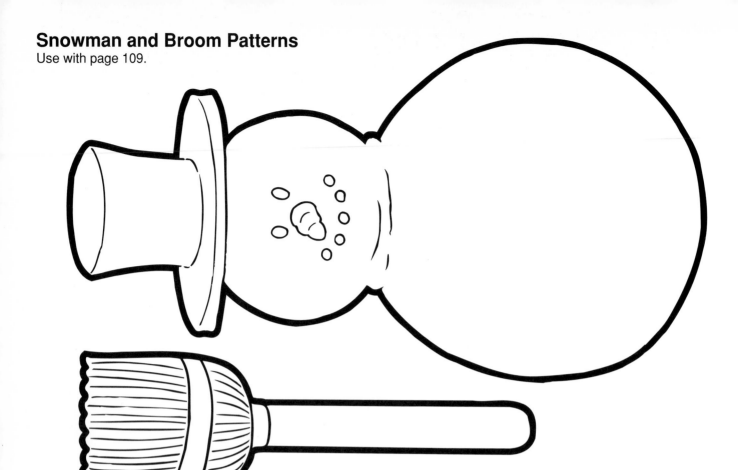

Name _____

_____ Survey

Survey

Questions	Directions	
1. Have you ever played in the snow?	Glue the snowman on	
A. yes		orange paper
B. no		yellow paper
2. Which do you wear on your head when it's cold?	Color the hat	
A. hat		red
B. earmuffs		green
C. neither		blue
3. Do you like hot chocolate?	Glue the broom on the	
A. yes		right side
B. no		left side
4. Which is your favorite winter activity?	Draw these buttons:	
A. sledding		⭘
B. ice-skating		△
C. building snowmen		☐
D. none of the above		●

Note to the teacher: Use with pages 108 and 109.

Names _____

Survey Question

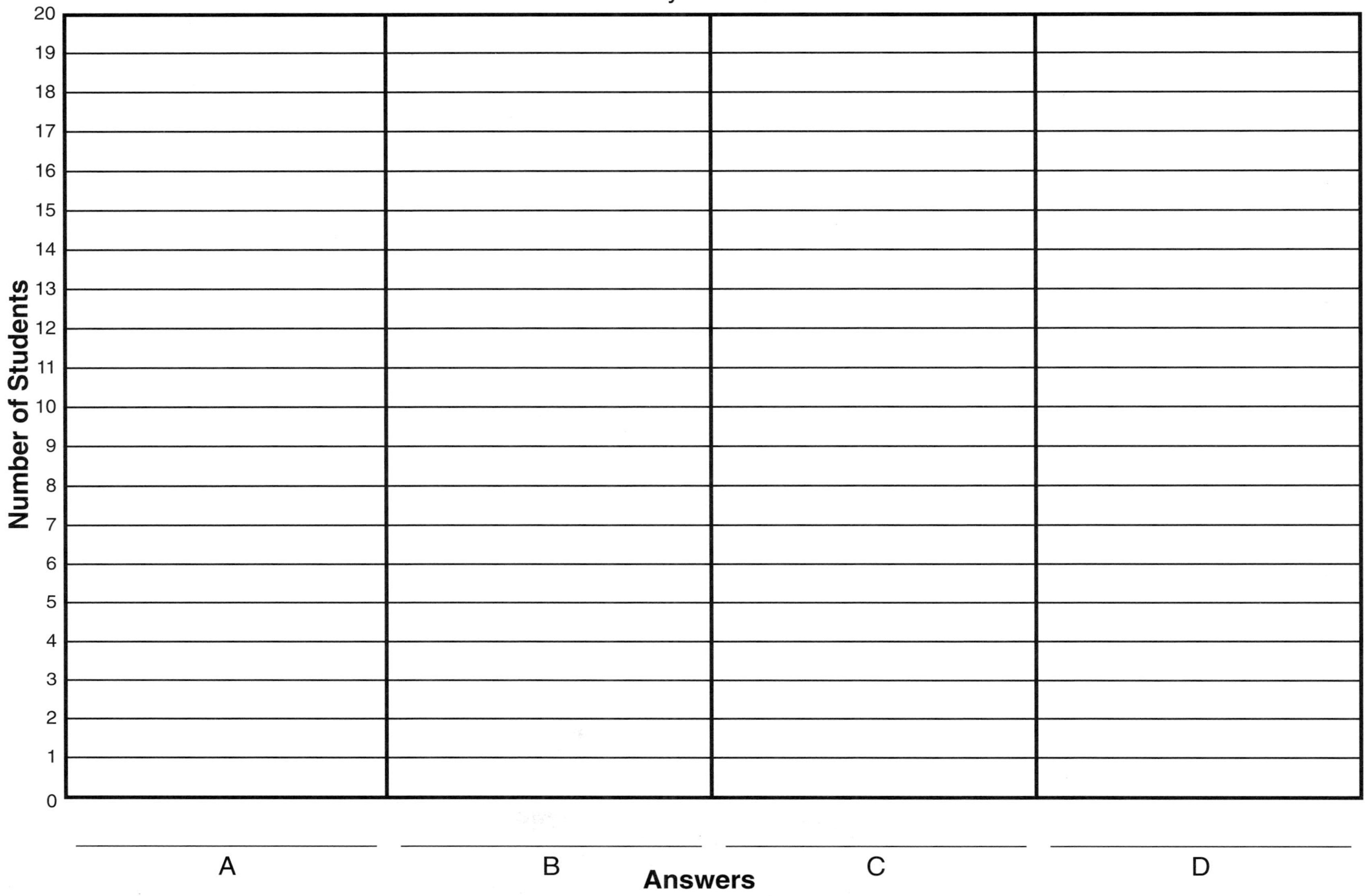

Number of Students

20				
19				
18				
17				
16				
15				
14				
13				
12				
11				
10				
9				
8				
7				
6				
5				
4				
3				
2				
1				
0				
	A	B	C	D

Answers

111

Note to the teacher: Use with "Extend It!" on page 109.

Hold Your Place

Looking for a novel way for students to display data? Have them create these dandy bookmarks, which double as glyphs!

Materials

- copy of the survey on page 114
- white construction paper copy of the glyph bookmark patterns on page 114
- copy of page 115
- scissors
- crayons
- access to a hole puncher
- access to white, yellow, and blue yarn

Name __Martin__   *Glyph guide*

A Preference for Reading

Circle one answer for each question.

Questions	Directions
1. Which do you prefer to read?	Cut out the
(nonfiction)	(oval)
fiction	rectangle
2. Which type of nonfiction do you prefer?	Color the bookmark
history	yellow
(science)	(red)
3. Which type of fiction do you prefer?	In the ◯ , draw
realistic	👤
(fantasy)	(☆)
4. Which is your favorite type of book character?	Draw this border:
person	∨∨∨∨∨
animal	∿∿∿
(thing)	(ℓℓℓℓℓℓℓ)
5. How often do you read for fun?	Knot this color yarn through the hole:
(once a week)	(white)
2 or more times a week	yellow
every day	blue

1. Introduce It!

Begin by informing students that a *glyph* uses a picture to display information, with each detail representing a different piece of data. Then tell students that they will be creating bookmark glyphs that show their reading preferences.

2. Collect It!

Tell students that before the glyphs can be constructed, information about the students' reading preferences must be gathered. Next, provide each child with a copy of the glyph guide on page 114. Tell him to write his name on the line provided. For each question, have him circle his reading preference along with the corresponding glyph direction.

3. Display It! Discuss It!

Give each child a white construction paper copy of the glyph bookmark patterns on page 114. Also confirm that he has access to the hole puncher and yarn. Tell him to cut out the bookmark that matches his response to question 1 and then hole-punch the top of the bookmark where indicated. Have him decorate his bookmark according to the rest of his responses on the glyph guide. Display the completed bookmark glyphs and glyph guide in a prominent place in the classroom. Invite students to study the glyphs and share any observations they have about their classmates' reading preferences. Call on volunteers to make true statements about the glyphs, such as "Michael's favorite book character is an animal," "Kassie reads every day," or "Tommy likes to read realistic fiction." Can you tell a reader by his bookmark? You bet!

4. Extend It!

This center activity shows students how their reading preferences compare with their classmates' preferences. Place student copies of page 115, the completed bookmark glyphs, and a copy of the glyph guide at a center. In turn, send each child to the center. Referring to his own glyph, instruct him to write his response to each question on the tally table. Then, for each response, tell him to find each of his classmate's glyphs that shows the same preference. Have him make a tally mark for each glyph in the corresponding space, and direct him to write the total.

Next, tell each child to write his preferences in the blanks along the bottom of the graph. For each one, have him color a bar to show the total number of students who share his preferences. Invite students to share their findings with the class. Encourage each student to place his bookmark in a book he is currently reading. What a novel idea!

Glyph Bookmark Patterns
Use with pages 112 and 113.

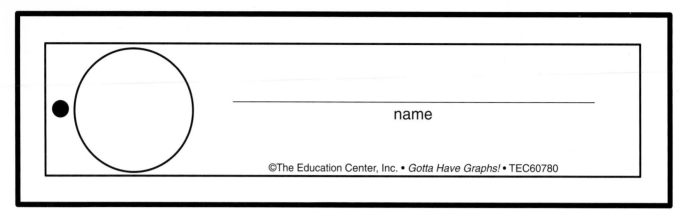

©The Education Center, Inc. • *Gotta Have Graphs!* • TEC60780

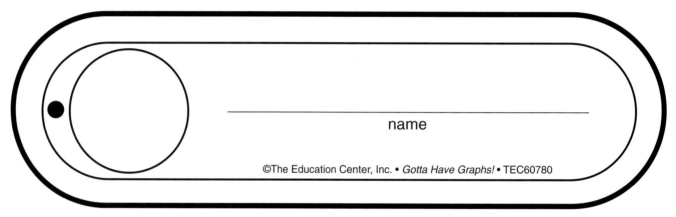

©The Education Center, Inc. • *Gotta Have Graphs!* • TEC60780

Name _____

Glyph guide

A Preference for Reading
Circle one answer for each question.

Questions	Directions
	Cut out the
1. Which do you prefer to read?	oval
nonfiction	rectangle
fiction	Color the bookmark
2. Which type of nonfiction do you prefer?	yellow
history	red
science	In the ◯, draw
3. Which type of fiction do you prefer?	✂
realistic	☆
fantasy	Draw this border:
4. Which is your favorite type of book character?	⋀⋀⋀⋀⋀
person	∿∿∿∿∿
animal	◖◖◖◖◖◖◖
thing	Knot this color yarn through the hole:
5. How often do you read for fun?	white
once a week	yellow
2 or more times a week	blue
every day	

©The Education Center, Inc. • *Gotta Have Graphs!* • TEC60780

Note to the teacher: Use with pages 112 and 113.

Who Agrees With Me?

Find your bookmark glyph.
Use it to write your reading preference for each question.
Then study your classmates' bookmark glyphs.
Make a tally mark for each student who has the same preference as you.
Then write each total.

Reading Preferences	Tally Marks	Total
1. Which do you prefer to read? _____		
2. Which type of nonfiction do you prefer? _____		
3. Which type of fiction do you prefer? _____		
4. Which is your favorite type of book character? _____		
5. How often do you read for fun?_____		

Study the tally table above.
Complete the bar graph below to show the results.

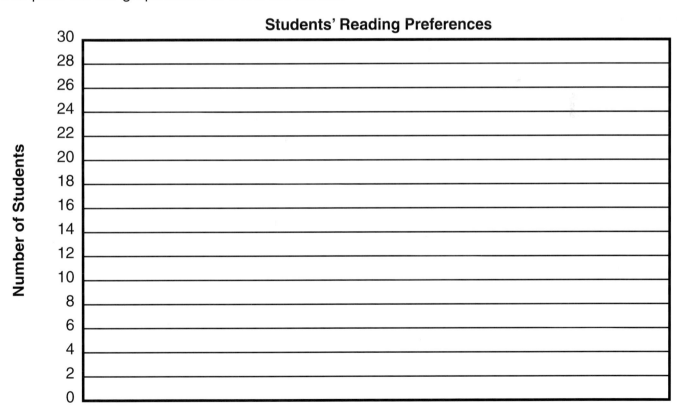

Students' Reading Preferences

Number of Students

30
28
26
24
22
20
18
16
14
12
10
8
6
4
2
0

Reading Preferences

"State-ly" Glyphs

When it comes to displaying state statistics, these glyphs do the trick!

Materials for Each Student

- copy of pages 118 and 119
- access to research materials (such as encyclopedias and approved Web sites)
- 9" x 12" sheet of construction paper
- black marker
- sticky notes

Hope

New Mexico

Name __Hope__ *Glyph*

State Statistics

State: __New Mexico__

1. Highest elevation: __13,161__ ft.
2. Statehood (order of admission into the Union): __47th__
3. Population: __1,819,046__
4. Electoral votes: __5__
5. Area: __121,599__ sq. mi.
6. Distribution: __73__ % urban
   __27__ % rural
7. Average July temperature: __74__ °F
8. Average January temperature: __34__ °F
9. Average yearly precipitation (rounded to the nearest five inches): __15__ in.

Name __Hope__ *Glyph*

State Glyph Guide

State: __New Mexico__

For each category, circle the statistics and corresponding glyph symbol for your state.

1. **Highest elevation (in feet) = body shape**	2. **Statehood = head shape**
2,000 or less = oval	1st–13th = diamond
2,001–10,000 = rectangle	14th–25th = circle
(10,001–20,000 = trapezoid)	26th–38th = triangle
20,001 or more = triangle	(39th–50th = square)

3. **Population = eyes**	4. **Electoral votes = nose**
1,000,000 or fewer	(10 or fewer =
(1,000,001–5,000,000)	11–20 =
5,000,001–10,000,000	21–30 =
10,000,001–20,000,000	31–40 =
20,000,001 or more	41–50 =
	51 or more =

5. **Area (in square miles) = mouth**	6. **Distribution = legs and feet**
10,000 or less	(100,001–150,000)	mostly urban =
10,001–50,000	150,001–200,000 =	mostly rural =
50,001–100,000	200,001 or more =	half urban, half rural =

7. **Average July temperature = position of arm on the left**	8. **Average January temperature = position of arm on the right**
81°F or above	66°F–70°F	51°F or above	21°F–30°F
76°F–80°F	61°F–65°F	41°F–50°F	11°F–20°F
(71°F–75°F)	60°F or below	(31°F–40°F)	10°F or below

9. **Average yearly precipitation = number of hairs on head**
   Draw 1 hair on the head for every 5 inches.

1. Introduce It!

Get this geographic activity off the ground by informing students that a *glyph* is a pictorial display of information. Each symbol in the picture represents information about the glyph subject. A glyph guide tells what each symbol means. Further explain that each student will create a glyph that displays the statistics for an assigned state.

2. Collect It!

In advance, arrange for student access to research materials that contain state data. (If desired, complete this section of the graphing unit in the school library.) Distribute student copies of "State Statistics" on page 118. Review the page with students. Next, assign each child a different state and have her write its name in the space provided. Instruct her to use the research materials to complete the information about her state.

Spencer

Pennsylvania

3. Display It! Discuss It!

To help each student make her state glyph, give her a 9" x 12" sheet of construction paper, a black marker, and a copy of page 119. Have her follow the directions on the page to identify the statistics and symbols for her state. Then tell her to use the symbols she has identified for her state to draw her glyph on the construction paper. Have her sign the top of her project. Then tell her to write the state name at the bottom so that her writing is visible from a distance. When students are finished, pair them. Then have each child tell about her partner's state by interpreting the glyph. Remind her to use the glyph guide to help her.

Next, guide each student to compare her state with others. To do this, display the completed glyphs for all students to see. Examine the glyphs as a class, leading students to discover any statistical trends. *(Possible trends include the following: The larger the population, the more electoral votes. The lower the January temperature, the lower the July temperature.)* Then give each child a copy of "'State-ly' Comparisons" on page 118. Have her follow the directions to list any states that have similar statistics. Remind her to use her glyph guide to help her. Prompt a discussion about the students' findings. Encourage students to identify states that have statistics most similar to their own.

4. Extend It!

How many states have fewer than 1 million residents? Within which range of July temperatures do most states fall? Lead students to study state statistics one category at a time with this symbolic graph activity! Confirm that each student has a glyph guide. Then, to prepare the graph, title and label a sheet of chart paper for a chosen statistic, such as area. Have each child jot her state name on a provided sticky note. Ask her to place the note above the corresponding category on the graph. Prompt a discussion about the results. Repeat this process with the remaining statistics as desired.

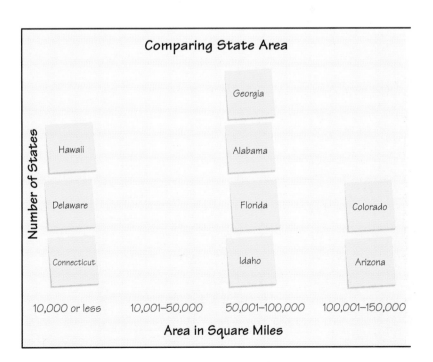

State Statistics

Glyph

Name _____

State: _____

1. Highest elevation: _____ ft.

2. Statehood (order of admission into the Union): _____

3. Population: _____

4. Electoral votes: _____

5. Area: _____ sq. mi.

6. Distribution: _____ % urban
   _____ % rural

7. Average July temperature: _____ °F

8. Average January temperature: _____ °F

9. Average yearly precipitation (rounded to the nearest five inches): _____ in.

©The Education Center, Inc. • *Gotta Have Graphs!* • TEC60780

"State-ly" Comparisons

Glyph

Name _____

My State: _____

For each category, look at the symbol for your state. Then study the other glyphs and find any identical symbols. Write the state names (up to three) on the lines provided.

Highest Elevation	Statehood
_____	_____
_____	_____
_____	_____

Population	Electoral Votes
_____	_____
_____	_____
_____	_____

Area	Distribution
_____	_____
_____	_____
_____	_____

Average July Temperature	Average January Temperature
_____	_____
_____	_____
_____	_____

Average Yearly Precipitation
_____
_____
_____

©The Education Center, Inc. • *Gotta Have Graphs!* • TEC60780

Note to the teacher: Use with pages 116 and 117.

State Glyph Guide

State: _____

For each category, circle the statistics and corresponding glyph symbol for your state.

1. Highest elevation (in feet) = body shape 2,000 or less = oval 2,001–10,000 = rectangle 10,001–20,000 = trapezoid 20,001 or more = triangle	**2. Statehood = head shape** 1st–13th = diamond 14th–25th = circle 26th–38th = triangle 39th–50th = square

3. Population = eyes

1,000,000 or fewer =

1,000,001–5,000,000 =

5,000,001–10,000,000 =

10,000,001–20,000,000 =

20,000,001 or more =

4. Electoral votes = nose

10 or fewer = ∧

11–20 = ⌒

21–30 = ○

31–40 = ●

41–50 = ∪

51 or more = ∨

5. Area (in square miles) = mouth

10,000 or less = ⌣   100,001–150,000 = ⩗⩗⩗

10,001–50,000 = ⌣⌣   150,001–200,000 = ⌣

50,001–100,000 = ∨   200,001 or more = ⌣

6. Distribution = legs and feet

mostly urban =

mostly rural =

half urban, half rural =

7. Average July temperature = position of arm on the left

81°F or above =   66°F–70°F =

76°F–80°F =   61°F–65°F =

71°F–75°F =   60°F or below =

8. Average January temperature = position of arm on the right

51°F or above =   21°F–30°F =

41°F–50°F =   11°F–20°F =

31°F–40°F =   10°F or below =

9. Average yearly precipitation = number of hairs on head

Draw 1 hair on the head for every 5 inches.

Clowning Around!

Wow your students with this fun Venn diagram activity!

Materials
- enlarged copy of page 122
- copy of page 123 for each pair
- scissors
- crayons
- glue

1. Introduce It!

Welcome students into the big top with this graphing activity. Begin by drawing two large overlapping circles on the board. Explain to students that the two circles are a part of a data display called a *Venn diagram.* Tell the class that these circles are for organizing the data they will collect about clowns named Larry and Sue.

Larry

Sue

Both

bow tie

smiling

flowers on shirt

pants

polka-dot hat

skirt

straight hair

shoes

curly hair

2. Collect It! Display It!

In advance, enlarge, color, and then cut out the clowns on page 122. Use the cutouts to label the Venn diagram as shown. Invite students to describe how Larry is different from Sue. Write their observations in the section labeled "Larry." Next, have students describe how Sue is different from Larry. Write their observations in the section labeled "Sue." Last, show students the overlapped area of the diagram. Explain that this area represents both clowns. Ask students to describe how the two clowns are alike and write their observations in the section labeled "Both."

3. Discuss It!

To check students' understanding of the collected data, ask a series of questions such as the ones listed below. Have each volunteer name the section of the diagram where the answer can be found, and invite him to read aloud the data shown there. To conclude, invite students to explain how organizing the data on a Venn diagram helped them compare the two clowns.

Questions
What does Larry have that Sue does not?
What does Sue have that Larry does not?
What do both clowns have in common?

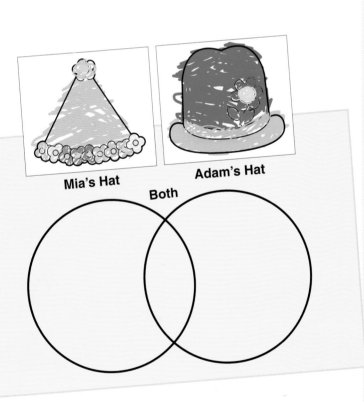

Mia's Hat   Adam's Hat
Both

4. Extend It!

For more clowning around with a Venn diagram, pair students and give each twosome a copy of page 123. Instruct one student in each pair to cut the page apart along the dotted line. Then have each child select a hat and color it as desired. Next, have the pair draw a Venn diagram on a 12" x 18" sheet of construction paper (provide seven-inch circle tracers if desired). Tell the pair to glue a hat above each circle and label the diagram. Allow time for students in each pair to take turns writing information about their hats in the appropriate sets on the diagram. Once completed, have pairs share their data with the class.

Clown Patterns

Use with pages 120 and 121.

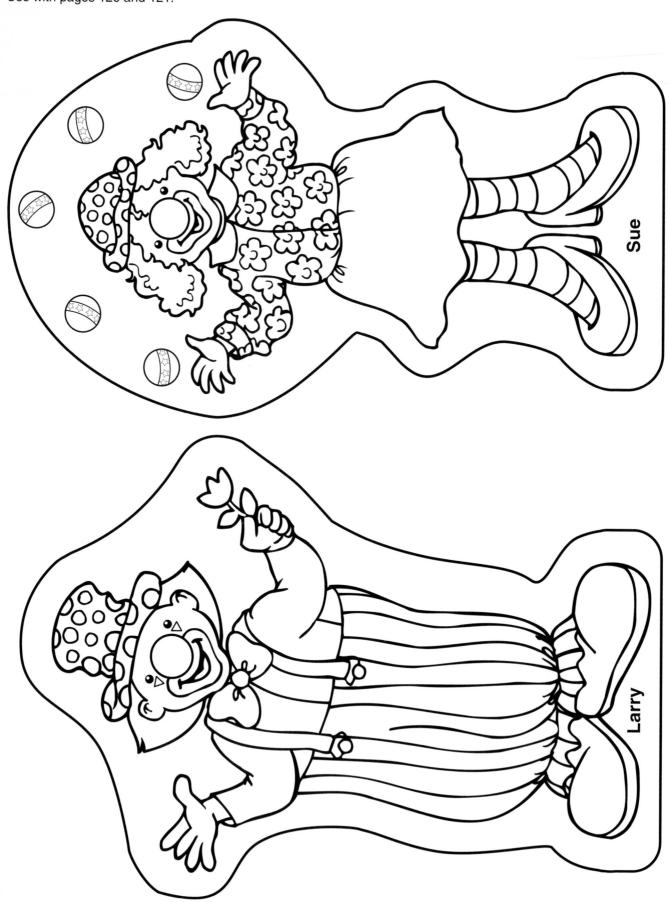

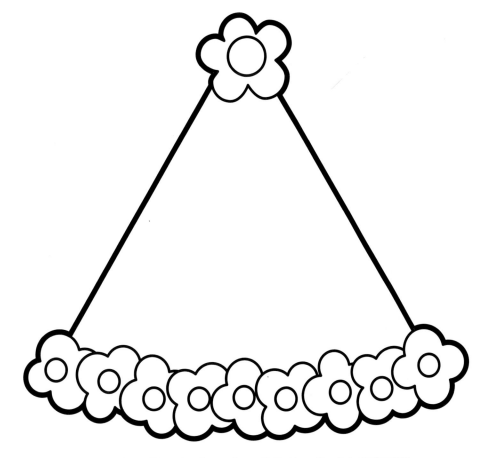

Movie Matters

Use this blockbuster to teach your film fans about Venn diagrams!

Materials
- copy of page 126 for each student
- copy of page 127 for each group
- crayons for each group

1. Introduce It!
To begin, ask student volunteers to name their favorite types of movies, what they like to eat at the movies, and whether they prefer to go to the movie theater or watch videos/DVDs at home. After students have shared, tell them that a helpful way to organize this information would be to use a *Venn diagram.* Inform students that this type of data display is used to compare and contrast things. It is represented by overlapping circles, each labeled for the data inside it. Unrelated data is placed outside the circles. Then tell students that they will be creating a Venn diagram about their movie preferences.

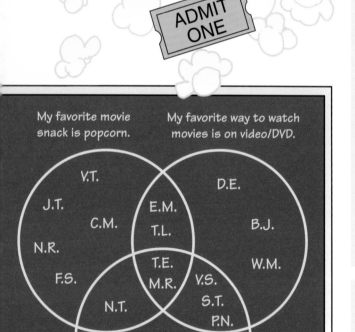

2. Collect It!
Draw a Venn diagram on the board and label it as shown. Read each statement and explain that the overlapping areas of the diagram indicate areas of more than one favorite. Then have each student, in turn, write her initials in the appropriate section to signify which statements apply to her. (Remind students that if none of the statements apply, the initials should be written outside of the circles.)

3. Display It! Discuss It!

Divide the class into small groups and give each student a copy of page 126. Direct each student to transfer the class information onto the page by marking in the appropriate section of the graph an X for each set of initials. Next, have her total each section and write the vote totals on the corresponding lines. Then have each group work together to answer the questions at the bottom of the reproducible. After each group has completed the questions, have students discuss the benefits of using a Venn diagram to display data. Lead students to conclude that this type of diagram displays a lot of information in a small space and is clear and easy to interpret.

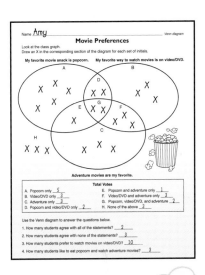

4. Extend It!

Determine which type of candy your moviegoers like to snack on during the show with this yummy bar graph activity. In turn, ask each child to name the candy she enjoys most while watching a movie. Write each item on the board as it is shared with the class, and group the responses into four categories—chocolate, gummy candy, hard candy, and other. Next, divide the class into three groups and give each group crayons and a copy of page 127. In turn, have each student write her name at the top of the reproducible and then color a box on her group's graph to indicate her favorite movie candy. On a large sheet of chart paper, draw a bar graph similar to the one shown. Gather the students and ask each group to report its data as you transfer the information onto the class graph. Lead a discussion about the differences, similarities, and benefits of both types of graphs. Chocolates, sweets, and treats—oh my!

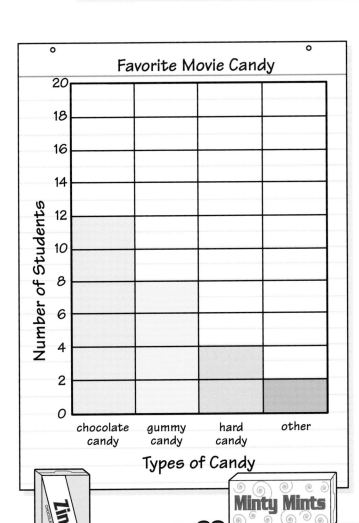

Movie Preferences

Look at the class graph.
Draw an X in the corresponding section of the diagram for each set of initials.

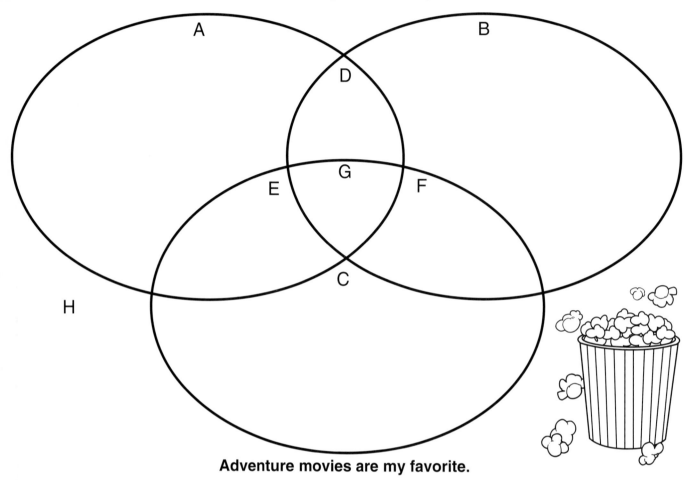

My favorite movie snack is popcorn.   **My favorite way to watch movies is on video/DVD.**

Adventure movies are my favorite.

Total Votes	
A. Popcorn only _____	E. Popcorn and adventure only _____
B. Video/DVD only _____	F. Video/DVD and adventure only _____
C. Adventure only _____	G. Popcorn, video/DVD, and adventure _____
D. Popcorn and video/DVD only _____	H. None of the above _____

Use the Venn diagram to answer the questions below.

1. How many students agree with all of the statements? _____

2. How many students agree with none of the statements? _____

3. How many students prefer to watch movies on video/DVD? _____

4. How many students like to eat popcorn and watch adventure movies? _____

Names ______________________________

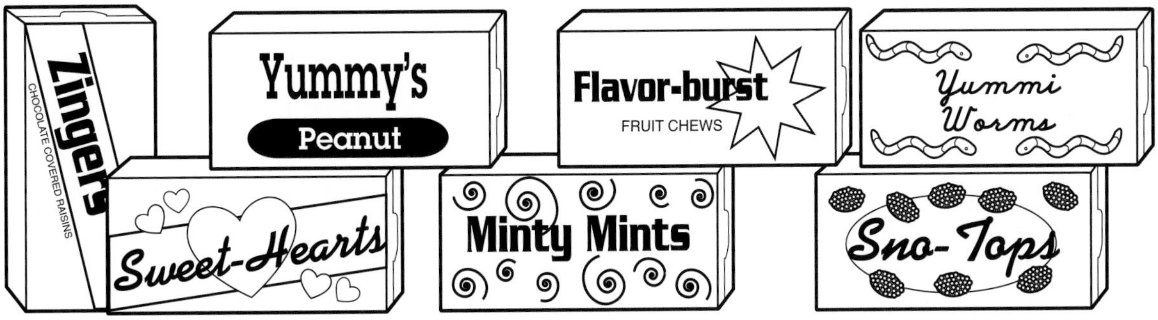

Zingers
CHOCOLATE COVERED RAISINS
Yummy's
Peanut
Flavor-burst
FRUIT CHEWS
Yummi Worms
Sweet-Hearts
Minty Mints
Sno-Tops

Favorite Movie Candy

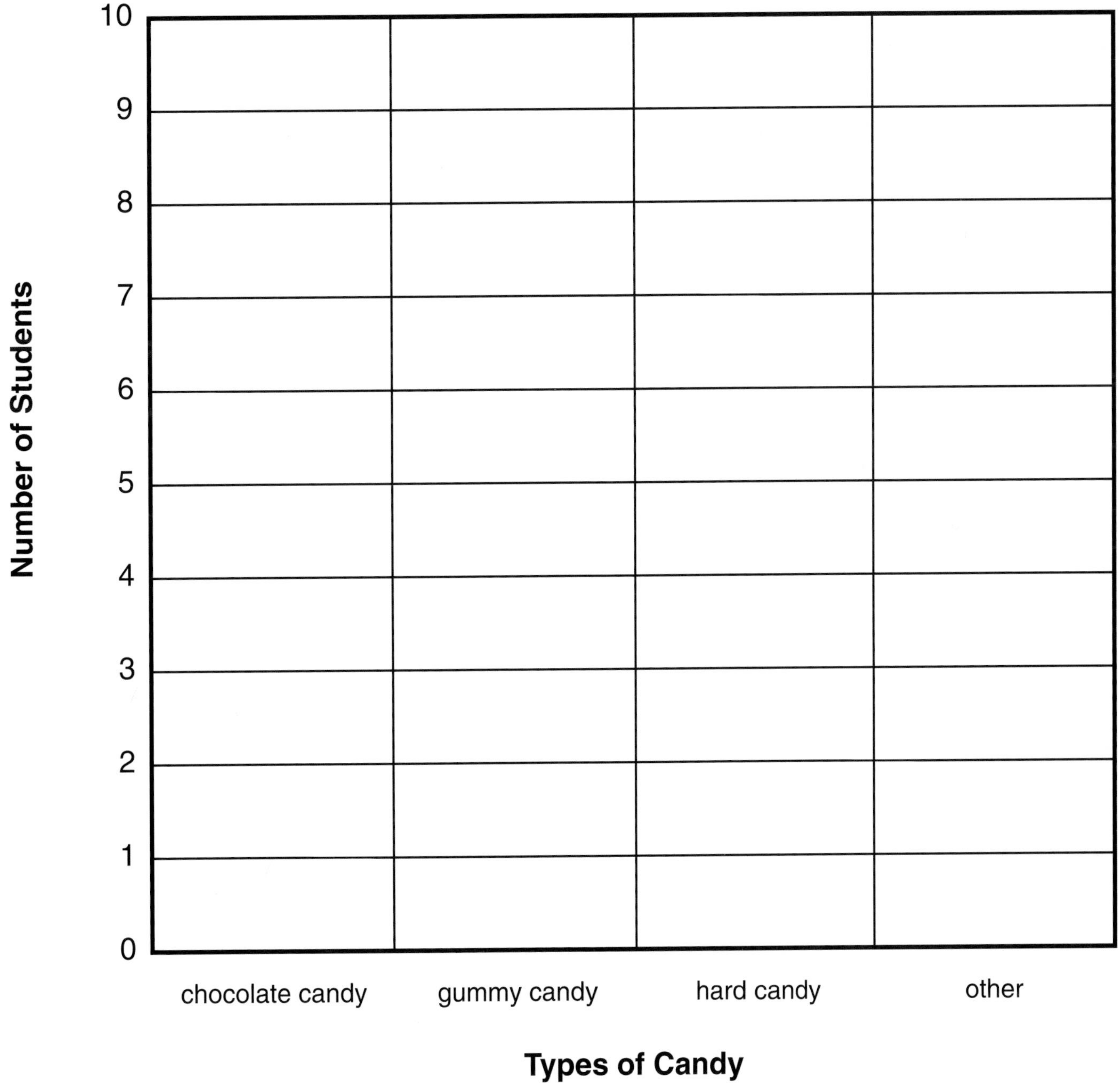

10
9
8
7
6
5
4
3
2
1
0
Number of Students
chocolate candy
gummy candy
hard candy
other
Types of Candy

Note to the teacher: Use with "Extend It!" on page 125.

All About Me!

Students get to know each other better in this "Venn-omenal" activity!

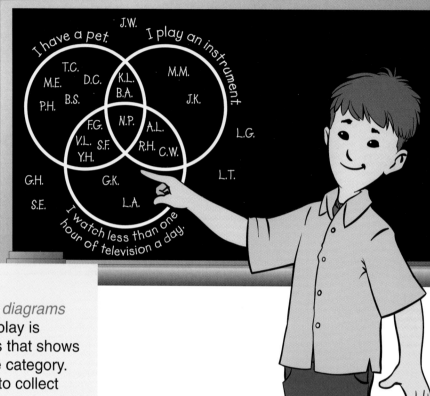

Materials
• copy of page 130
• copy of page 131

1. Introduce It!

Get students acquainted with *Venn diagrams* by explaining that this type of data display is made up of a set of intersecting circles that shows how data can belong in more than one category. Explain that the diagram can be used to collect and display data.

Venn Diagram Statements

I have a pet.
I was born in this state.
I play an instrument.
I play on a sports team.
I watch less than one hour of television a day.
I like ice cream.
I am a member of a club.
I like pizza.
I have a hobby.

2. Collect It! Display It!

To get started, draw a three-circle Venn diagram on the board. Label each circle with a different statement (see the suggestions). Read each statement and inform students that each child will write his initials in the appropriate area to indicate which statements (if any) apply to him. Then give each student a copy of page 130. Have him label his version of the Venn diagram with the statements. Next, ask the student to predict which statement or combination of statements applies to the majority of students. Have him draw a star beside the letter for that set. Also have him predict which set applies to the fewest students and make a check mark beside the letter for that set. Then, on the Venn diagram you drew on the board, invite each student to initial the appropriate set to indicate which statements apply to him. (If none of the statements apply, have the student place his initials outside of the circles.) Remind students that placing their initials inside sections of overlapping circles means that two or more of the statements apply to them.

3. Discuss It!

After each student has initialed the class Venn diagram, count the initials inside and outside each set. Direct students to record each number on their diagrams in the corresponding spaces. Ask each child to compare his prediction with the results and write about the results at the bottom of the reproducible. Next, lead students to draw conclusions about the data with questions such as the following: How many students initialed the same set as you did? How many students have a pet? What fraction of the class plays an instrument and watches less than one hour of television a day?

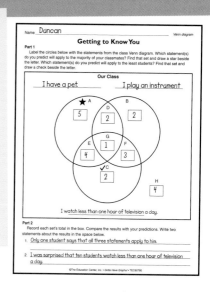

4. Extend It!

Give students the chance to share more about themselves by having them collect data on their own Venn diagrams. Enlist students' help in brainstorming a list of statements that tell about them. Then provide each student with a copy of page 131. Direct him to label each circle with a statement that describes him, referring to the brainstormed list if desired. (Remind him to select statements that are also likely to apply to some of his classmates.) Explain that each student will read each classmate's diagram and mark an X in the section (if any) that describes him. Before beginning the rotation, have each student make a prediction about the results of his own diagram. Have him record his prediction on the back of the page. Then tell each student to place his diagram faceup on his desk and mark his own X.

Next, have students follow an established classroom path to visit each desk. For each diagram, tell the student to mark an X to show which statements apply to him. When students return to their desks, ask each child to study his diagram and compare the results with his prediction. Then have him write two statements that describe his data in the space provided. Finally, guide a class discussion to determine what students learned about their classmates.

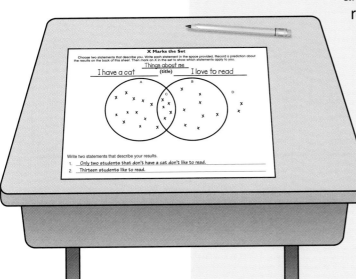

Name _____

Getting to Know You

Part 1

Label the circles below with the statements from the class Venn diagram. Which statement(s) do you predict will apply to the majority of your classmates? Find that set and draw a star beside the letter. Which statement(s) do you predict will apply to the least students? Find that set and draw a check beside the letter.

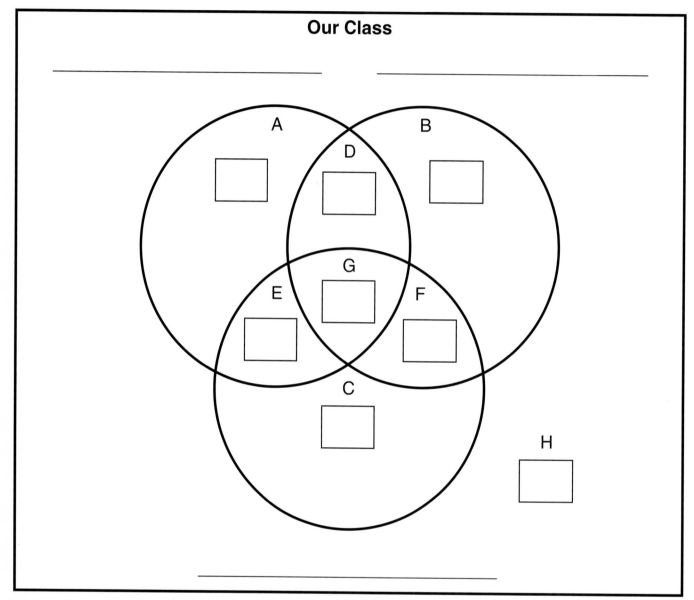

Part 2

Record each set's total in the box. Compare the results with your predictions. Write two statements about the results in the space below.

1. _____

_____

2. _____

_____

Name _____

X Marks the Set

Choose two statements that describe you. Write each statement in the space provided. Record a prediction about the results on the back of this sheet. Then mark an X in the set to show which statements apply to you.

_____
(title)

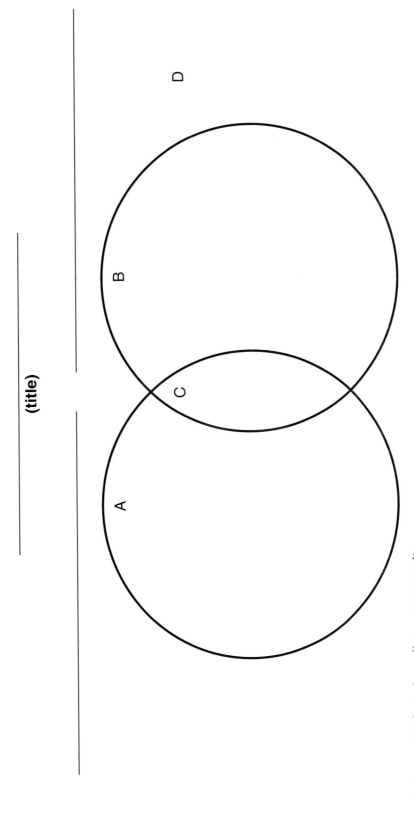

Write two statements that describe your results.

1. _____

2. _____

©The Education Center, Inc. • *Gotta Have Graphs!* • TEC60780

Note to the teacher: Use with "Extend It!" on page 129.

131

The Timelines of Our Lives

Students recall important events in their lives with this biographical timeline activity.

Materials

- programmed copy of page 134 and a bar graph from page 135 for each student
- large piece of bulletin board paper for each group
- marker for each group
- programmed sentence strip for each group
- scissors
- crayons
- glue

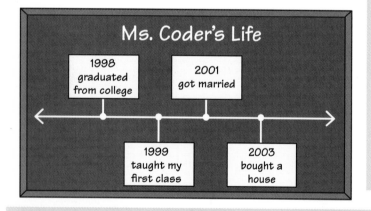

Ms. Coder's Life

1998 graduated from college

2001 got married

1999 taught my first class

2003 bought a house

1. Introduce It!

Introduce students to *timelines* as they look back on important childhood events! On the board, create a simple timeline of important events in your life similar to the one shown. Begin by explaining that a timeline is a graph that is on a number line. It shows some measure of time, such as days, weeks, months, or years. After sharing your timeline with students, explain that they will be constructing a similar display about important things that have happened in their lives.

2. Collect It!

Enlist help from home to collect data for the timelines. Make a copy of page 134 and program the note with a return date. Distribute student copies of the page. In addition, create a number line on a sentence strip for each group of six students. To do this, trace the center line of the strip with a black marker. Number the line, beginning with the earliest birth year of your students and ending with the current year. Be sure to alternate writing the years above and below the line. (See the sample.)

After the completed event cards have been returned, ask each child to cut them out along the bold lines. Divide students into groups of six. Provide each group with crayons, glue, a marker, a number line, and a large piece of bulletin board paper. Have each child share her events with the members of her group. Then ask her to select one event for her group's timeline.

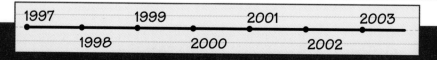

3. Display It! Discuss It!

Tell each group to create its timeline by gluing its sentence strip on the horizontally positioned bulletin board paper. Have each group member vertically align her event card with the corresponding year on the timeline, alternating the cards above and below the strip and placing event cards from the same year in columns as shown. After all the cards have been placed, tell the group members to space the cards apart evenly and glue them in place. Then tell each group member to draw a line connecting her card to the corresponding year (or to another card) as shown. Have each group add a title above its timeline.

Invite each group to share its timeline with the class. Ask questions about events using time-related vocabulary such as *before, after, earliest,* and *latest.* After all the timelines have been shared, display them at students' eye level for later viewing.

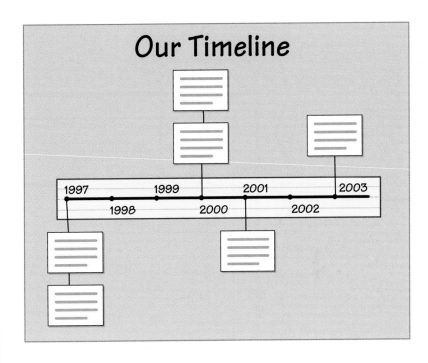

4. Extend It!

To further students' study of the events, try this bar graph activity. On a copy of page 135, label the bottom of each bar graph with time spans appropriate for the years represented by students' timelines (such as "1997 to 1999" and "2000 to 2003"). Give each child a copy of a bar graph. Have her refer to her group's timeline to determine how many events fall within each span of years. Tell her to color the corresponding spaces on the graph. Invite students to discuss the results as a class.

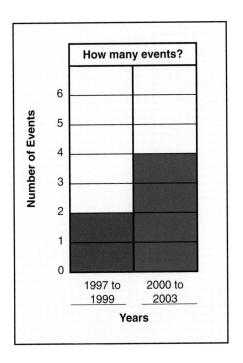

Dear Family,

　　We are learning about timelines at school. On each card below, help your child write about an important event from his or her life and the year it happened. We will use this information to create timelines about our lives. Please return this paper to school by _____. Thank you!

Name _____

Event _____

_____

_____
Year

Name _____

Event _____

_____

_____
Year

Name _____

Timely Events

Study the timeline.
Color the bar graph to show when each event happened.

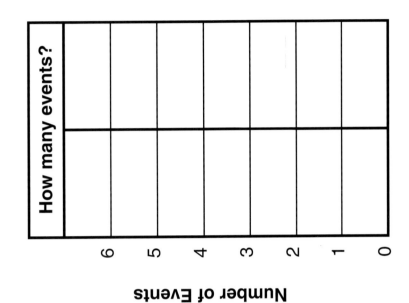

How many events?	
6	
5	
4	
3	
2	
1	
0	

Number of Events

Years _____

Name _____

Timely Events

Study the timeline.
Color the bar graph to show when each event happened.

How many events?	
6	
5	
4	
3	
2	
1	
0	

Number of Events

Years _____

Note to the teacher: Use with "Extend It!" on page 133.

Once Upon a Timeline

Students will love investigating the publishing dates of their favorite picture books with this timeline activity.

Materials

- copy of the book pattern on page 138 for each student
- construction paper copies of the headline cards on page 139
- bulletin board space designated for the timeline
- index cards
- push pins
- sentence strip
- yarn
- discarded newspapers
- scissors
- glue
- masking tape

1. Introduce It!

To begin, have students recall their favorite picture books. Invite them to think about books they currently enjoy reading or books their parents read to them when they were younger. Ask them to guess how long ago the books were written. Then inform students that they will create a class *timeline* to show when their favorite books were first published. Remind students that a timeline is a graph that is on a number line. It shows some measure of time, such as days, weeks, months, or years.

2. Collect It!

In advance, arrange for each child to select a favorite picture book and bring it to class by a designated date. Then, to prepare for the timeline, mount a length of yarn horizontally across the length of a bulletin board. To begin, give each child a copy of a book pattern from page 138. Explain how to locate the book's publishing date on the copyright page. (Stress to students that they should find the earliest date.) Have each student write the book's title, the publishing date, and his name in the space provided on the book pattern.

One Cool Day
Title

1989
Date Published

Timothy
Student's Name

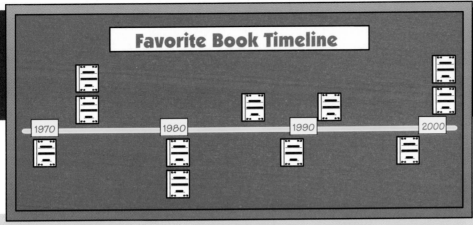

Favorite Book Timeline

3. Display It! Discuss It!

Determine as a class the earliest and latest publishing dates. Program index cards with the corresponding decades. (For example, if the dates are 1977 and 1999, program cards for 1970, 1980, 1990, and 2000.) Mount the cards along the timeline, spacing them apart evenly. Then, using the push pins, guide students to display their book patterns along the timeline sequentially, alternating patterns above and below the yarn and stacking patterns with identical publishing dates. Use a sentence strip to add the title "Favorite Book Timeline." Then invite students to study the time-line. Use the provided questions to help students draw conclusions about the results.

Questions

What is the earliest date a book was published? What is the most recent date a book was published?

Were most students' favorite books published before, after, or around the same time you were born?

In which year or span of years were the most books published?

How might the timeline be different if it showed the publishing dates for your parents' favorite books? *(Possible answer: The dates would probably be earlier.)*

Extend It!

This growing timeline will make headlines! Collect discarded newspapers for a two-week period. Tape a length of yarn across a classroom wall. Then program a different index card for each date and mount them in chronological order atop the yarn. Place a roll of masking tape, the newspapers, construction paper copies of the headline cards on page 139, and glue nearby. Direct a child to locate a headline of his choice during his free time. Have him write his name and the newspaper's date on a headline card. Then tell him to cut out the headline and glue it in the space provided, cutting apart the words and reassembling them as needed to fit the space. Have him use a loop of masking tape to mount the card below the corresponding date. When there is at least one headline for each date, study the timeline as a class. Lead students to acknowledge any ongoing stories based on the headlines and identify the types of stories featured (such as local, national, and world news). What a scoop!

Wednesday, March 5

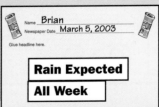

Name Brian
Newspaper Date March 5, 2003
Glue headline here.

Rain Expected
All Week

Book Patterns

Use with pages 136 and 137.

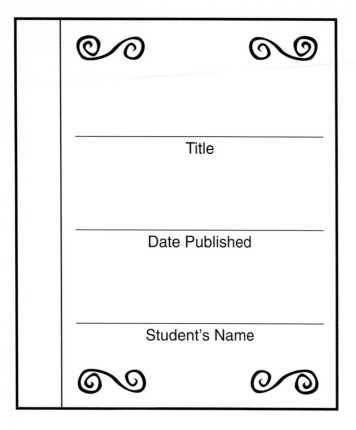

Title

Date Published

Student's Name

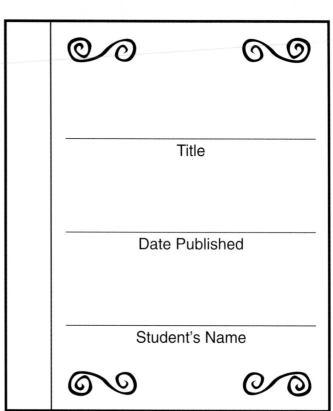

Title

Date Published

Student's Name

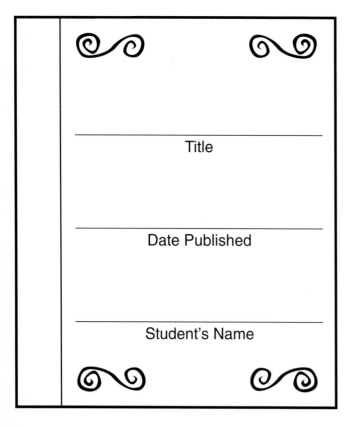

Title

Date Published

Student's Name

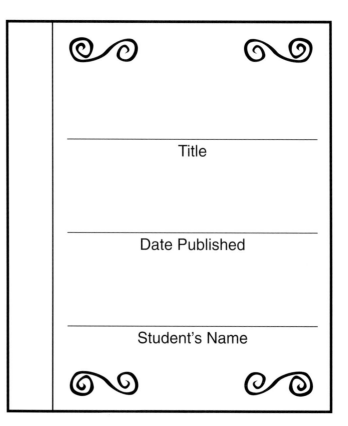

Title

Date Published

Student's Name

Name _____

Newspaper Date_____

Glue headline here.

Name _____

Newspaper Date_____

Glue headline here.

A Lively Timeline

Help students look at the past, present, and future with this timeline activity.

By 2033, I plan to be president!

Materials for Each Student

- 2 tagboard copies of page 142
- copy of page 143
- supply of ½" x 6" tagboard strips
- access to a stapler
- quarter sheets of drawing paper
- sentence strip
- ruler
- crayons
- scissors
- glue

1. Introduce It!

To begin this timely activity, inform students that a *timeline* displays chronological data on a number line. The numbers on the graph represent some measure of time, such as hours, days, or years. Clarify that timelines can show both past and planned future events. Then explain that each student will create a timeline that shows events from her childhood as well as her future plans.

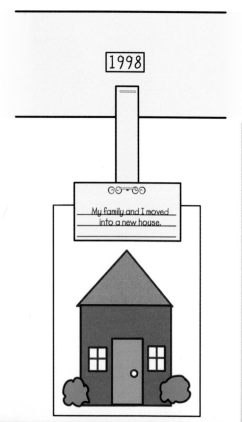

1998

My family and I moved into a new house.

2. Collect It! Display It!

To help students prepare their timelines, give each child two tagboard copies of page 142. Have her cut out the patterns along the bold lines. Then, on each of a desired number of the event cards, have her write about a memorable childhood event or a future aspiration for a different year of her life. Invite her to illustrate some of the events on quarter sheets of drawing paper. Instruct her to glue each sheet to the corresponding event card as shown.

Next, have each student glue the four timeline strips together. Tell her to program the boxes with consecutive years, beginning with the year she was born. To suspend each event card, direct her to staple a tagboard strip so that it hangs down vertically from the appropriate date on the timeline. Then instruct her to staple the top of the event card to the bottom of the strip as shown.

3. Discuss It!

Next, invite each student to share her timeline with the class. Prompt the class to discuss her past and future events by asking questions such as the following: How old was [student's name] when she moved into a new house? How many years after she started playing piano did she have her first recital? At what age does she plan to make her first million dollars? After each student has had a chance to share her work, display the timelines for everyone to see.

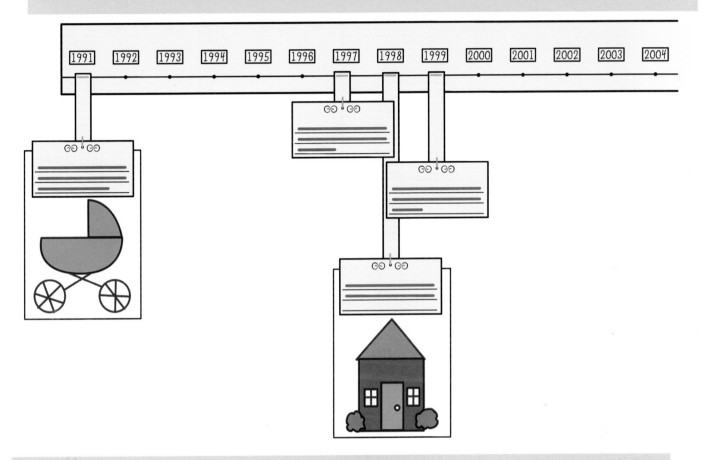

4. Extend It!

Students will agree—people-watching provides interesting data for a timeline! As a class, brainstorm a list of situations in which students might track a person's actions, such as a parent's time after work, a soccer game, or a baby-sitting experience. Give each student a copy of page 143. Instruct her to record a selected person's name and the corresponding situation in the space provided, followed by the time period in which the person will be observed. Then have the student program the chart with appropriate increments of time. (Explain that she does not need to use all the spaces.)

To complete the chart, instruct each student to take her recording sheet home and jot down her observations during each time period. Upon returning to class, give each student a sentence strip and a ruler. Tell her to title the strip and then label it with the corresponding times to make a timeline similar to the one shown. Then have her program the timeline with her observations. Provide time for each student to share her work with the class.

Timeline and Event Cards

Use with pages 140 and 141.

Glue here.

Glue here.

A Day in the Life Of...

In the space below, write the name of the person you will observe, the event or situation, and the time frame. Write the time increments in the chart. (You do not need to use all the spaces.) Then record your observations.

I will observe _____ from ____:____ to ____:____.

(person and event/situation)

Time	Observation	Time	Observation

Gotta Have Graphs!

35 Kid-Pleasing, Curriculum-Based Graphing and Data Display Lessons

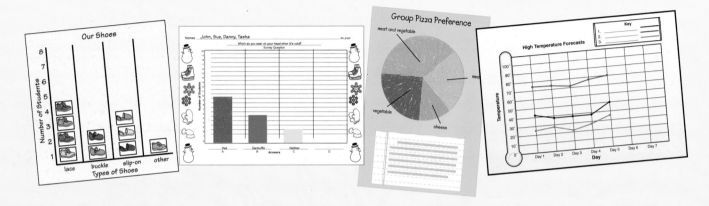

Managing Editor: Denine T. Carter
Assistant Managing Editors: Kelly Coder, Kelli L. Gowdy
Editor at Large: Diane Badden
Staff Editors: Sherry McGregor, Peggy W. Hambright
Contributing Writers: Amy Barsanti, Lisa Buchholz, Ann Hefflin, Cynthia Holcomb, Starin Lewis, Diane F. McGraw, Laura Mihalenko, Kim Minafo, Valerie Wood Smith, Laura Wagner, Brenda Wilke, Joyce Wilson
Copy Editors: Tazmen Carlisle, Amy Kirtley-Hill, Karen L. Mayworth, Kristy Parton, Debbie Shoffner, Cathy Edwards Simrell
Cover Artists: Pam Crane, Clevell Harris
Art Coordinator: Clevell Harris
Artists: Pam Crane, Theresa Lewis Goode, Clevell Harris, Ivy L. Koonce, Clint Moore, Greg D. Rieves, Rebecca Saunders, Barry Slate, Stuart Smith, Donna K. Teal
The Mailbox® Books.com: Jennifer Tipton Bennett (DESIGNER/ARTIST); Karen White (INTERNET COORDINATOR); Paul Fleetwood, Xiaoyun Wu (SYSTEMS)

President, The Mailbox Book Company™: Joseph C. Bucci
Director of Book Planning and Development: Chris Poindexter
Curriculum Director: Karen P. Shelton
Book Development Managers: Cayce Guiliano, Elizabeth H. Lindsay, Thad McLaurin
Editorial Planning: Kimberley Bruck (MANAGER); Debra Liverman, Sharon Murphy, Susan Walker (TEAM LEADERS)
Editorial and Freelance Management: Karen A. Brudnak; Sarah Hamblet, Hope Rodgers (EDITORIAL ASSISTANTS)
Editorial Production: Lisa K. Pitts (TRAFFIC MANAGER); Lynette Dickerson (TYPE SYSTEMS); Mark Rainey (TYPESETTER)
Librarian: Dorothy C. McKinney